SELECTED ESSAYS

SELECTED ESSAYS

KARL MARX

Translator:- H. J. Stenning

Serenity
Publishers, LLC

ROCKVILLE, MARYLAND
2008

ISBN: 978-1-60450-511-5

Published by Serenity Publishers
An Arc Manor Company
P. O. Box 10339
Rockville, MD 20849-0339
www.SerenityPublishers.com

Printed in the United States of America/United Kingdom

CONTENTS

PREFACE

The present volume consists of a translation of some of Karl Marx's principal writings during the six years 1844-1850.

In 1843 Marx was twenty-five years old. He had just married, apparently on the strength of the modest salary he was to receive for editing, jointly with Arnold Ruge, a periodical called the *Deutsch-Franzoesische Jahrbuecher (Franco-German Annuals)*, the purpose of which was to promote the union of German philosophy with French social science. Only one double-number of this journal appeared in 1844. It contained Marx's criticism of the Hegelian Philosophy of Right and his exposition of the social significance of the Jewish question, in the form of a review of two works by Bruno Bauer.

Translations of both articles are given in this volume.

They possess a special interest for the Marxian student, as they exhibit the grafting of a materialist philosophy upon the idealist philosophy of Hegel, and show the employment of the Hegelian dialectic in the investigation of political and historical questions.

It was not long before Marx and Ruge became intellectually estranged, and the third essay, "The King of Prussia and Social Reform," which appeared in the Paris socialist journal *Vorwaerts*, contains a severe polemic against Ruge. In the same organ Marx published an elaborate defence of Engels in particular and communists in general from the strictures of Karl

Heinzen, a radical republican politician. In both essays Marx ranges over a wide field, and develops his own views upon economic, political and historical questions.

The essay on Proudhon emphasizes the special merits of that writer as a pioneer of economic criticism, and forms a counterweight to Marx's devastating criticism of Proudhon in the "Poverty of Philosophy." This piece and the sketch of French materialism are extracted from *Die Heilige Familie (The Holy Family)*, a comprehensive work of satirical criticism, in which Marx and Engels (whose share in writing the book was a very small one), settled accounts with their philosophic conscience.

The critique of the views of M. Guizot upon the English and French middle-class revolutions appeared in the *Neue Rhenische Revue (New Rhenish Review)*, a periodical which Marx and Engels edited from London in 1850.

H.J.S.

A CRITICISM OF THE HEGELIAN PHILOSOPHY OF RIGHT

A s far as Germany is concerned the criticism of religion is practically completed, and the criticism of religion is the basis of all criticism.

The profane existence of error is threatened when its heavenly *oratio pro aris et focis*[1] has been refuted.

He who has only found a reflexion of himself in the fantastic reality of heaven where he looked for a superman, will no longer be willing to find only the semblance of himself, only the sub-human, where he seeks and ought to find his own reality.

The foundation of the criticism of religion is: Man makes religion, religion does not make man. Religion indeed is man's self-consciousness and self-estimation while he has not found his feet in the universe. But Man is no abstract being, squatting outside the world. Man is the world of men, the State, society. This State, this society produces religion, which is an inverted world-consciousness, because they are an inverted world. Religion is the general theory of this world, its encyclopædic compendium, its logic in popular form, its spiritualistic *Point d'honneur*, its enthusiasm, its moral sanction, its solemn complement, its general basis of consolation and justification. It is the fantastic realization of the human being, inasmuch as the human being possesses no true reality. The struggle against

---

1   Speech in defence of hearths and homes.

9

religion is therefore indirectly the struggle against that world whose spiritual aroma is religion.

Religious misery is in one mouth the expression of real misery, and in another is a protestation against real misery. Religion is the moan of the oppressed creature, the sentiment of a heartless world, as it is the spirit of spiritless conditions. It is the opium of the people.

The abolition of religion, as the illusory happiness of the people, is the demand for their real happiness. The demand to abandon the illusions about their condition is a demand to abandon a condition which requires illusions. The criticism of religion therefore contains potentially the criticism of the Vale of Tears whose aureole is religion.

Criticism has plucked the imaginary flowers which adorned the chain, not that man should wear his fetters denuded of fanciful embellishment, but that he should throw off the chain, and break the living flower.

The criticism of religion disillusions man, so that he thinks, acts, shapes his reality like the disillusioned man come to his senses, so that he revolves around himself, and thus around his real sun. Religion is but the illusory sun which revolves around man, so long as he does not revolve around himself.

It is therefore the task of history, once the *thither* side of truth has vanished, to establish the truth of the *hither* side.

The immediate task of philosophy, when enlisted in the service of history, is to unmask human self-alienation in its unholy shape, now that it has been unmasked in its holy shape. Thus the criticism of heaven transforms itself into the criticism of earth, the criticism of religion into the criticism of right, and the criticism of theology into the criticism of politics.

The following essay—a contribution to this work—is in the first place joined not to the original, but to a copy, to the German philosophy of politics and of right, for no other reason than because it pertains to Germany.

If one should desire to strike a point of contact with the German *status quo*, albeit in the only appropriate way, which
is negatively, the result would ever remain an anachronism.
Even the denial of our political present is already a dust-cov-
ered fact in the historical lumber room of modern nations. If
I deny the powdered wig, I still have to deal with unpowdered
wigs. If I deny the German conditions of 1843, I stand, according to French chronology, scarcely in the year 1789, let alone in
the focus of the present.

German history flatters itself that it has a movement which
no people in the historical heaven have either executed before
or will execute after it. We have in point of fact shared in the
restoration epoch of modern nations without participating in
their revolutions.

We were restored, in the first place, because other nations
dared to make a revolution, and, in the second place, because
other nations suffered a counter revolution: in the first place,
because our masters were afraid, and, in the second place, because they regained their courage.

Led by our shepherds, we suddenly found ourselves in the society of freedom on the day of its interment.

As a school which legitimates the baseness of to-day by the
baseness of yesterday, a school which explains every cry of the
serf against the knout as rebellious, once the knout becomes a
prescriptive, a derivative, a historical knout, a school to which
history only shows itself *a posteriori,* like the God of Israel to
his servant Moses, the historical juridical school would have
invented German history, were it not itself an invention of
German history.

On the other hand, good-humoured enthusiasts, Teutoma-
niacs by upbringing and freethinkers by reflexion, seek for
our history of freedom beyond our history in the Teutonic
primeval woods. But in what respect is our freedom history
distinguished from the freedom history of the boar, if it is
only to be found in the woods? Moreover, as one shouts into
the wood, so one's voice comes back in answer ("As the ques-

11

tion, so the answer"). Therefore peace to the Teutonic primeval woods.

But war to German conditions, at all events! They lie below the level of history, they are liable to all criticism, but they remain a subject for criticism just as the criminal who is below the level of humanity remains a subject for the executioner.

Grappling with them, criticism is no passion of the head, it is the head of passion. It is no anatomical knife, it is a weapon. Its object is its enemy, which it will not refute but destroy. For the spirit of the conditions has been refuted. In and for themselves they are no memorable objects, but existences as contemptible as they are despised. Criticism has already settled all accounts with this subject. It no longer figures as an end in itself, but only as a means. Its essential pathos is indignation, its essential work is denunciation.

What we have to do is to describe a series of social spheres, all exercising a somewhat sluggish pressure upon each other, a general state of inactive dejection, a limitation which recognizes itself as much as it misunderstands itself, squeezed within the framework of a governmental system, which, living on the conservation of all meannesses, is itself nothing less than meanness in government.

What a spectacle! On the one hand, the infinitely ramified division of society into the most varied races, which confront each other with small antipathies, bad consciences, and brutal mediocrity, and precisely because of the ambiguous and suspicious positions which they occupy towards each other, such positions being devoid of all real distinctions although coupled with various formalities, are treated by their lords as existences on sufferance. And even more. The fact that they are ruled, governed, and owned they must acknowledge and confess as a favour of heaven! On the other hand, there are those rulers themselves whose greatness is in inverse proportion to their number.

The criticism which addresses itself to this object is criticism in hand-to-hand fighting, and in hand-to-hand fighting, it is not a question of whether the opponent is a noble opponent, of equal birth, or an interesting opponent; it is a question of meeting him. It is thus imperative that the Germans should have no opportunity for self-deception and resignation. The real pressure must be made more oppressive by making men conscious of the pressure, and the disgrace more disgraceful by publishing it.

Every sphere of German society must be described as the *partie honteuse*[2] of German society, these petrified conditions must be made to dance by singing to them their own melody! The people must be taught to be startled at their own appearance, in order to implant courage into them.

And even for modern nations this struggle against the narrow-minded actuality of the German *status quo* cannot be without interest, for the German *status quo* represents the frank completion of the *ancien régime*, and the *ancien régime* is the concealed defect of the modern State. The struggle against the German political present is the struggle against the past of modern nations, which are still vexed by the recollections of this past. For them it is instructive to see the *ancien régime,* which enacted its tragedy with them, playing its comedy as the German *revenant.* Its history was tragic so long as it was the pre-existing power of the world, and freedom, on the other hand, a personal invasion, in a word, so long as it believed and was obliged to believe in its justification. So long as the *ancien régime* as the existing world order struggled with a nascent world, historical error was on its side, but not personal perversity. Its downfall was therefore tragic.

On the other hand, the present German régime, which is an anachronism, a flagrant contradiction of the generally recognized axiom of the obsolescence of the *ancien régime,* imagines that it believes in itself, and extorts from the world the same homage. If it believed in its own being, would it seek to hide it under the semblance of an alien being and look for its salvation in hypocrisy and sophistry? The modern *ancien ré-*

---

2   Shameful part.

gime is merely the comedian of a world order whose real heroes are dead.

History is thorough, and passes through many phases when it bears an old figure to the grave. The last phase of a world historical figure is its comedy. The gods of Greece, once tragically wounded to death in the chained Prometheus of Æschylus, were fated to die a comic death in Lucian's dialogues. Why does history take this course? In order that mankind may break away in a jolly mood from its past.

In the light of this historical foresight, the political powers of Germany are vindicated. As soon then as the modern politico-social reality is itself subjected to criticism, as soon, therefore, as criticism raises itself to the height of truly human problems, it either finds itself outside the German *status quo*, or it would delve beneath the latter to find its object.

To take an example! The relation of industry, and of the world of wealth generally, to the political world is one of the chief problems of modern times. Under what form is this problem beginning to engage the attention of Germans? Under the form of protective tariffs, of the system of prohibition, of political economy. Teutomania has passed out of men and gone into matter, and thus one fine day we saw our cotton knights and iron heroes transformed into patriots. Thus in Germany we are beginning to recognize the sovereignty of monopoly at home, in order that it may be invested with sovereignty abroad. We are now beginning in Germany at the point where they are leaving off in France and England.

The old rotten condition, against which these countries are theoretically in revolt, and which they only tolerate as chains are borne, is greeted in Germany as the dawning of a splendid future, which as yet scarcely dares to translate itself from cunning[3] theory into the most ruthless practice. Whereas the problem in France and England reads: Political economy or the rule of society over wealth, it reads in

---

3   *listigen*, a play on the name of the protectionist economist F. List.

Germany: national economy or the rule of private property over nationality. Thus England and France are faced with the question of abolishing monopoly which has been carried to its highest point; in Germany the question is to carry monopoly to its highest point.

If, therefore, the total German development were not in advance of the political German development, a German could at the most take part in present-day problems only in the same way as a Russian can do so.

But if the individual is not bound by the ties of a nation, the entire nation is even less liberated by the emancipation of an individual. The Scythians made no advance towards Greek culture because Greece numbered a Scythian among her philosophers. Luckily we Germans are no Scythians.

As the old nations lived their previous history in imagination, in mythology, so we Germans live our history to come in thought, in philosophy. We are philosophical contemporaries of the present without being its historical contemporaries. German philosophy is the ideal prolongation of German history. If, therefore, we criticize the *œuvres posthumes* of our ideal history, philosophy, instead of the *œuvres incomplète-sof our real history, our criticism occupies a position among the questions of which the present says: *that is the question.*[4] That which represents the decaying elements of practical life among the progressive nations with modern State conditions first of all becomes critical decay in the philosophical reflexion of these conditions in Germany, where the conditions themselves do not yet exist.

German juridical and political philosophy is the sole element of German history which stands *al pari* with the official modern present.

The German people must therefore strike this their dream history against their existing conditions, and subject to criticism not only these conditions, but at the same time their abstract continuation.

4   In English in the original.

Their future can neither be confined to the direct denial of their real nor to the direct enforcement of their ideal political and juridical conditions, for they possess the direct denial of their real conditions in their ideal conditions, and the direct enforcement of their ideal conditions they have almost out-lived in the opinion of neighbouring nations. Consequently the practical political party in Germany properly demands the negation of philosophy. Its error consists not in the demand, but in sticking to the demand, which seriously it neither does nor can enforce. It believes it can accomplish this negation by turning its back on philosophy, the while its averted head utters a few irritable and banal phrases over it. Moreover, its horizon is so limited as to exclude philosophy from the realm of German actuality unless it imagines philosophy to be implied in German practice and in the theories subserving it. It urges the necessity for linking up with vital forces, but forgets that the real vital force of the German people has hitherto only pullulated under its skull.

In a word: you cannot abolish philosophy without putting it into practice. The same error, only with the factors reversed, is committed by the theoretical party, the political party which founds on philosophy.

The latter perceives in the present struggle only the critical struggle of philosophy with the German world; it does not suspect that all previous philosophy has itself been a part of this world, and is its complement, if an ideal one. While critical towards its opposing party, it behaves uncritically towards itself. It starts from the assumptions of philosophy, but either refuses to carry further the results yielded by philosophy, or claims as the direct outcome of philosophy results and demands which have been culled from another sphere.

We reserve to ourselves a more detailed examination of this party.

Its fundamental defect may be reduced to this: it believes it can enforce philosophy without abolishing it. The criticism of German juridical and political philosophy, which has received through Hegel its most consistent, most ample and most recent shape, is at once both the critical analysis of the modern State and of the actuality which is connected therewith, and in addition the decisive repudiation of the entire previous mode of the German political and juridical consciousness, whose principal and most universal expression, elevated to the level of a science, is speculative jurisprudence itself.

While, on the one hand, speculative jurisprudence, this abstract and exuberant thought-process of the modern State, is possible only in Germany, on the other hand, the German conception of the modern State, making abstraction of real men, was only possible because and in so far as the modern State itself makes abstraction of real men or only satisfies the whole of man in an imaginary manner.

Germans have thought in politics what other peoples have done. Germany was *their* theoretical conscience. The abstraction and arrogance of her thought always kept an even pace with the one-sidedness and stunted growth of her actuality. If, therefore, the *status quo* of the German civic community expresses the completion of the *ancien régime*, the completion of the pile driven into the flesh of the modern State, the *status quo* of German political science expresses the inadequacy of the modern State, the decay that is set up in its flesh.

As a decisive counterpart of the previous mode of German political consciousness, the criticism of speculative jurisprudence does not run back upon itself, but assumes the shape of problems for whose solution there is only one means: practice.

The question arises: can Germany attain to a practice *à la hauteur de principes,*[5] that is, to a revolution which will not only raise her to the level of modern nations, but to the human level which will be the immediate future of these nations?

The weapon of criticism cannot in any case replace the criticism of weapons, material force must be overthrown by material force, but theory too becomes a material force as soon as it grasps weapons. Theory is capable of grasping weapons

5   In conformity with principles.

17

as soon as its argument becomes *ad hommine,* and its argument becomes *ad hominem* as soon as it becomes radical. To be radical is to grasp the matter by its root. Now the root for mankind is man himself. The evident proof of the radicalism of German theory, and therefore of its practical energy, is its outcome from the decisive and positive abolition of religion.

The criticism of religion ends with the doctrine that man is the supreme being for mankind, and therefore with the categorical imperative to overthrow all conditions in which man is a degraded, servile, neglected, contemptible being, conditions which cannot be better described than by the exclamation of a Frenchman on the occasion of a projected dog tax: "Poor dogs; they want to treat you like men!"

Even historically, theoretical emancipation has a specifically practical significance for Germany. Germany's revolutionary past is particularly theoretical, it is the Reformation. Then it was the monk, and now it is the philosopher in whose brain the revolution begins.

Luther vanquished servility based upon devotion, because he replaced it by servility based upon conviction. He shattered faith in authority, because he restored the authority of faith. He transformed parsons into laymen, because he transformed laymen into parsons. He liberated men from outward religiosity, because he made religiosity an inward affair of the heart. He emancipated the body from chains, because he laid chains upon the heart.

But if Protestantism is not the true solution, it was the true formulation of the problem. The question was no longer a struggle between the layman and the parson external to him; it was a struggle with his own inner parson, his parsonic nature. And if the protestant transformation of German laymen into parsons emancipated the lay popes, the princes, together with their clergy, the privileged and the philistines, the philosophic transformation of the parsonic Germans into men will emancipate the people. But little as emancipation stops short of the princes, just as little will the secularization of property stop short of church robbery, which was chiefly set on foot by the hypocritical Prussians. Then the Peasants' War, the most radical fact of German history, came to grief on the reef of theology. To-day, when theology itself has come to grief, the most servile fact of German history, our *status quo*, will be shivered on the rock of philosophy.

The day before the Reformation, official Germany was the most abject vassal of Rome. The day before its revolution, it is the abject vassal of less than Rome, of Prussia and Austria, of country squires and philistines.

Meanwhile there seems to be an important obstacle to a radical German revolution.

Revolutions in fact require a passive element, a material foundation.

Theory becomes realized among a people only in so far as it represents the realization of that people's needs. Will the immense cleavage between the demands of the German intellect and the responses of German actuality now involve a similar cleavage of middle-class society from the State, and from itself? Will theoretical needs merge directly into practical needs? It is not enough that the ideas press towards realization; reality itself must stimulate to thinking.

But Germany did not pass through the middle stages of political emancipation simultaneously with the modern nations. Even the stages which she has overcome theoretically she has not reached practically.

How would she be able to clear with a *salto mortale* not only her own obstacles, but at the same time the obstacles of modern nations, obstacles which she must actually feel to mean a liberation to be striven for from her real obstacles? A radical revolution can only be the revolution of radical needs, whose preliminary conditions appear to be wholly lacking.

Although Germany has only accompanied the development of nations with the abstract activity of thought, without taking an active part in the real struggles incident to this development, she has, on the other hand, shared in the suffering incident to this development, without sharing in its enjoyments, or their partial satisfaction. Abstract activity on the one side corresponds to abstract suffering on the other side.

Consequently, one fine day Germany will find herself at the level of European decay, before she has ever stood at the level of European emancipation. The phenomenon may be likened to a fetish-worshipper, who succumbs to the diseases of Christianity.

Looking upon German governments, we find that, owing to contemporary conditions, the situation of Germany, the standpoint of German culture and finally their own lucky instincts, they are driven to combine the civilized shortcomings of the modern State world, whose advantages we do not possess, with the barbarous shortcomings of the *ancien régime*, which we enjoy in full measure, so that Germany is constantly obliged to participate, if not intelligently, at any rate unintelligently, in the State formations which lie beyond her *status quo*.

Is there for example a country in the world which shares so naively in all the illusions of the constitutional community, without sharing in its realities, as does so-called constitutional Germany? Was it necessary to combine German governmental interference, the tortures of the censorship, with the tortures of the French September laws which presupposed freedom of the press? Just as one found the gods of all nations in the Roman pantheon, so will one find the flaws of all State forms in the Holy Roman German Empire. That this eclecticism will reach a point hitherto unsuspected is guaranteed in particular by the politico-æsthetic *gourmanderie* of a German king, who thinks he can play all the parts of monarchy, both of the feudal and the bureaucratic, both of the absolute and the constitutional, of the autocratic as of the democratic, if not in the person of his people, then in his own person, if not for the people, then for himself. Germany as the embodiment of the defect of the political present, constituted in her own world, will not be able to overthrow the specifically German obstacles without overthrowing the general obstacles of the political present.

It is not the radical revolution which is a utopian dream for Germany, not the general human emancipation, but rather the partial, the merely political revolution, the revolution which leaves the pillars of the house standing. Upon what can a partial, a merely political revolution base itself? Upon the fact that a part of bourgeois society could emancipate itself and attain to general rulership, upon the fact that, by virtue of its special situation, a particular class could undertake the general emancipation of society. This class would liberate the whole of society, but only upon the assumption that the whole of society found itself in the situation of this class, and consequently possessed money and education, for instance, or could acquire them if it liked.

No class in bourgeois society can play this part without setting up a wave of enthusiasm in itself and among the masses, a wave of feeling wherein it would fraternize and commingle with society in general, and would feel and be recognized as society's general representative, a wave of enthusiasm wherein its claims and rights would be in truth the claims and rights of society itself, wherein it would really be the social head and the social heart. Only in the name of the general rights of society can a particular class vindicate for itself the general rulership.

Revolutionary energy and intellectual self-confidence are not sufficient by themselves to enable a class to attain to this emancipatory position, and thereby exploit politically all social spheres in the interest of its own sphere. In order that the revolution of a people should coincide with the emancipation of a special class of bourgeois society, it is necessary for a class to stand out as a class representing the whole of society. Thus further involves, as its obverse side, the concentration of all the defects of society in another class, and this particular class must be the embodiment of the general social obstacles and impediments. A particular social sphere must be identical with the notorious crime of society as a whole, in such wise that the emancipation of this sphere would appear to be the general self-emancipation. In order that one class should be the class of emancipation *par excellence,* another class must contrariwise be the class of manifest subjugation. The negative-general significance of the French nobility and the French clergy was the condition of the positive-general significance of the class of the bourgeoisie, which was immediately encroaching upon and confronting the former.

But in Germany every class lacks not only the consistency, the keenness, the courage, the ruthlessness, which might stamp it as the negative representative of society. It lacks equally that breadth of soul which would identify it, if only momentarily, with the popular soul, that quality of genius which animates material power until it becomes political power, that revolutionary boldness which hurls at the opponent the defiant words: I am nothing, and I have to be everything. But the stock-in-trade of German morality and honour, not only as regards individuals but also as regards classes, constitutes rather that modest species of egoism which brings into prominence its own limitations.

The relation of the various spheres of German society is therefore not dramatic, but epic. Each of them begins to be self-conscious and to press its special claims upon the others not when it is itself oppressed, but when the conditions of the time, irrespective of its co-operation, create a sociable foundation from which it can on its part practise oppression. Even the moral self-esteem of the German middle class is only based on the consciousness of being the general representative of the philistine mediocrity of all the other classes.

Consequently it is not only the German kings who succeed to the throne *mal à propos,* but it is every sphere of bourgeois society which experiences its defeat before it celebrates its victory, develops its own handicaps before it overcomes the handicaps which confront it, asserts its own narrow-minded nature before it can assert its generous nature, so that even the opportunity of playing a great part is always past before it actually existed, and each class, so soon as it embarks on a struggle with the class above it, becomes involved in a struggle with the class below it. Consequently, the princedom finds itself fighting the monarchy, the bureaucrat finds himself fighting the nobility, the bourgeois finds himself fighting them all, while the proletariat is already commencing to fight the bourgeois.

The middle class hardly dares to seize hold of the ideas of emancipation from its own standpoint before the development of social conditions and the progress of political theory declare this standpoint to be antiquated, or at least very problematical. In France partial emancipation is the basis of universal emancipation. In Germany universal emancipation is the *conditio sine qua non* of every partial emancipation. In France it is the reality, in Germany it is the impossibility of gradual emancipation which must bring forth entire freedom. In France every popular class is tinged with political idealism, and does not feel primarily as a particular class, but as the representative of social needs generally. The role of emancipator, therefore, flits from one class to another of the French people in a dramatic movement, until it eventually reaches the class which will no longer realize social freedom upon the basis of certain conditions lying outside of mankind and yet created by human society, but will rather organize all the conditions of human existence upon the basis of social freedom. In Germany, on the other hand, where practical life is as unintellectual as intellectual life is unpractical, no class of bourgeois society either feels the need or possesses the capacity for emancipation, unless driven thereto by its immediate position, by material necessity, by its chains themselves.

Wherein, therefore, lies the positive possibility of German emancipation?

Answer: In the formation of a class in radical chains, a class which finds itself in bourgeois society, but which is not of it, an order which shall break up all orders, a sphere which possesses a universal character by virtue of its universal suffering, which lays claim to no special right, because no particular wrong but wrong in general is committed upon it, which can no longer invoke a historical title, but only a human title, which stands not in a one-sided antagonism to the consequences, but in a many-sided antagonism to the assumptions of the German community, a sphere finally which cannot emancipate itself without emancipating all the other spheres of society, which represents in a word the complete loss of mankind, and can therefore only redeem itself through the complete redemption of mankind. The dissolution of society reduced to a special order is the proletariat.

The proletariat arises in Germany only with the beginning of the industrial movement; for it is not poverty resulting from natural circumstances but poverty artificially created, not the masses who are held down by the weight of the social system, but the multitude released by the acute break-up of society—especially of the middle class—which gives rise to the proletariat. When the proletariat proclaims the dissolution of the existing order of things it is merely announcing the secret of its own existence, for it is in itself the virtual dissolution of this order of things. When the proletariat desires the negation of private property, it is merely elevating to a general principle of society what it already involuntarily embodies in itself as the negative product of society.

With respect to the nascent world the proletariat finds itself in the same position as the German king occupies with respect to the departed world, when he calls the people his people, just as he calls a horse his horse. In declaring the people to be his private property, the king acknowledges that private property is king.

Just as philosophy finds in the proletariat its material weapons, so the proletariat finds in philosophy its intellectual weapons, and as soon as the lightning of thought has penetrated into the flaccid popular soil, the elevation of Germans into men will be accomplished.

Let us summarize the result at which we have arrived. The only liberation of Germany that is practical or possible is a liberation from the standpoint of the theory that declares man to be the supreme being of mankind. In Germany emancipation from the Middle Ages can only be effected by means of emancipation from the results of a partial freedom from the Middle Ages. In Germany no brand of serfdom can be extirpated without extirpating every kind of serfdom. Fundamental Germany cannot be revolutionized without a revolution in its basis. The emancipation of Germans is the emancipation of mankind. The head of this emancipation is philosophy; its heart is the proletariat. Philosophy cannot be realized without the abolition of the proletariat, the proletariat cannot abolish itself without realizing philosophy.

When all the inner conditions are fulfilled, the German day of resurrection will be announced by the crowing of the Gallic Cock.

ON THE JEWISH QUESTION

1. BRUNO BAUER, *Die Judenfrage (The Jewish Question),*
   Brunswick 1843.

2. BRUNO BAUER, *Die Faehigkeit der heutigen Juden und*
   Christen, frei zu werden (The Capacity of Modern Jews
   and Christians to become free), Zurich 1843.

1. BRUNO BAUER, *Die Judenfrage,* Brunswick 1843.

The German Jews crave for emancipation. What emancipation
do they crave? Civic, political emancipation.

Bruno Bauer answers them: Nobody in Germany is politically
emancipated. We ourselves are unfree. How shall we liberate
you? You Jews are egoists, if you demand a special emancipation for yourselves as Jews. As Germans you ought to labour
for the political emancipation of Germany, as men for human
emancipation, and you ought to feel the special nature of your
oppression and your disgrace not as an exception from the
rule, but rather as its confirmation.

Or do Jews demand to be put on an equal footing with Christian subjects? Then they recognize the Christian State as justified, then they recognize the régime of general subjugation.
Why are they displeased at their special yoke, when the gen-

eral yoke pleases them? Why should Germans interest themselves in the emancipation of the Jews, if Jews do not interest themselves in the emancipation of Germans?

The Christian State knows only privileges. In that State the Jew possesses the privilege of being a Jew. As a Jew, he has rights which a Christian has not. Why does he crave the rights which he has not, and which Christians enjoy?

If the Jew wants to be emancipated from the Christian State, then he should demand that the Christian State abandon its religious prejudice. Will the Jew abandon his religious prejudice? Has he therefore the right to demand of another this abdication of religion?

By its very nature the Christian State cannot emancipate the Jews; but, adds Bauer, by his very nature the Jew cannot be emancipated.

So long as the State is Christian and the Jew is Jewish, both are equally incapable of granting and receiving emancipation.

The Christian State can only behave towards the Jew in the manner of a Christian State, that is in a privileged manner, by granting the separation of the Jew from the other subjects, but causing him to feel the pressure of the other separated spheres, and all the more onerously inasmuch as the Jew is in religious antagonism to the dominant religion. But the Jew also can only conduct himself towards the State in a Jewish fashion, that is as a stranger, by opposing his chimerical nationality to the real nationality, his illusory law to the real law, by imagining that his separation from humanity is justified, by abstaining on principle from all participation in the historical movement, by waiting on a future which has nothing in common with the general future of mankind, by regarding himself as a member of the Jewish people and the Jewish people as the chosen people.

Upon what grounds therefore do you Jews crave emancipation? On account of your religion? It is the mortal enemy of the State religion. As citizens? There are no citizens in Germany. As men? You are as little men as He on whom you called.

After giving a criticism of the previous positions and solutions of the question, Bauer has freshly posited the question of Jewish emancipation. How, he asks, are they constituted, the Jew to be emancipated, and the Christian State which is to emancipate? He replies by a criticism of the Jewish religion, he analyses the religious antagonism between Judaism and Christianity, he explains the nature of the Christian State, and all this with boldness, acuteness, spirit, and thoroughness, in a style as precise as it is forcible and energetic.

How then does Bauer solve the Jewish question? What is the result? The formulation of a question is its solution. The criticism of the Jewish question is the answer to the Jewish question.

The summary is therefore as follows:

We must emancipate ourselves before we are able to emancipate others.

The most rigid form of the antagonism between the Jew and the Christian is the religious antagonism. How is this antagonism resolved? By making it impossible. How is a religious antagonism made impossible? By abolishing religion.

As soon as Jew and Christian recognize their respective religions as different stages in the development of the human mind, as different snake skins which history has cast off, and men as the snakes encased therein, they stand no longer in a religious relationship, but in a critical, a scientific, a human one. Science then constitutes their unity. Antagonisms in science, however, are resolved by science itself.

The German Jew is particularly affected by the lack of political emancipation in general and the pronounced Christianity of the State. In Bauer's sense, however, the Jewish question has a general significance independent of the specific German conditions.

It is the question of the relation of religion to the State, of the contradiction between religious entanglement and political emancipation. Emancipation from religion is posited as a condition, both for the Jews, who desire to be politically emancipated, and for the State, which shall emancipate and itself be emancipated.

"Good, you say, and the Jew says so too, the Jew also is not to be emancipated as Jew, not because he is a Jew, not because he has such an excellent, general, human principle of morality; the Jew will rather retire behind the citizen and be a citizen, although he is a Jew and wants to remain one: that is, he is and remains a Jew, in spite of the fact that he is a citizen and lives in general human relationships: his Jewish and limited nature always and eventually triumphs over his human and political obligations. The prejudice remains in spite of the fact that it has been outstripped by general principles. If, however, it remains, it rather outstrips everything else." "Only sophistically and to outward seeming would the Jew be able to remain a Jew in civic life; if he desired to remain a Jew, the mere semblance would therefore be the essential thing and would triumph, that is, his life in the State would be only a semblance or a passing exception to the rule and the nature of things" ("The Capacity of modern Jews and Christians to become free," p. 57).

Let us see, on the other hand, how Bauer describes the task of the State: "France has recently (proceedings of the Chamber of Deputies, 26th December 1840) in connection with the Jewish question—as constantly in all other political questions—given us a glimpse of a life which is free, but revokes its freedom in law, and therefore asserts it to be a sham, and on the other hand contradicts its free law by its act." "The Jewish Question," p. 64.

"General freedom is not yet legal in France, the Jewish question is not yet solved, because legal freedom—that all citizens are equal—is limited in practice, which is still dominated by religious privileges, and this unfreedom in practice reacts on the law, compelling the latter to sanction the division of nominally free citizens into oppressed and oppressor," p. 65.

When, therefore, would the Jewish problem be solved for France?

"The Jew, for instance, must cease to be a Jew if he will not allow himself to be hindered by his law from fulfilling his duties towards the State and his fellow-citizens, going, for example, to the Chamber of Deputies on the Sabbath and taking part in the public sittings. Every religious privilege, and consequently the monopoly of a privileged Church, must be surrendered, and if few or many or even the great majority believe they ought still to perform religious duties, this performance must be left to themselves as a private matter," p. 65. "When there is no longer a privileged religion, there will no longer be a religion. Take from religion its excommunicating power, and it exists no longer," p. 66.

On the one hand, Bauer states that the Jew must abandon Judaism, and that man must abandon religion, in order to be emancipated as a citizen. On the other hand, he feels he is logical in interpreting the political abolition of religion to mean the abolition of religion altogether. The State, which presupposes religion, is as yet no true, no real State. "At any rate the religious idea gives the State guarantees. But what State? What kind of State?" p. 97.

At this point we are brought up against the one-sided conception of the Jewish question.

It was by no means sufficient to inquire: Who shall emancipate? Who shall be emancipated? Criticism had a third task to perform.

It had to ask: what kind of emancipation are we concerned with? Upon what conditions is the desired emancipation based? The criticism of political emancipation itself was only the eventual criticism of the Jewish question and its true solution, in the "general question of the time."

Because Bauer does not raise the question to this level he falls into contradictions. He posits conditions which are not involved in the nature of political emancipation itself. He suggests questions which his problem does not imply, and he solves problems which leave his questions unsettled. Whereas Bauer says of the opponents of Jewish emancipation: "Their mistake was that they assumed the Christian State to be the only real State, and did not subject it to the same criticism that they applied to Judaism," we find Bauer's mistake to consist in the fact that it is only the Christian State, and not the "general State," that he subjects to criticism, that he does not investigate the relation of political emancipation to human emancipation, and consequently lays down conditions which are only explicable from an uncritical confusion of political emancipation with general human emancipation.

When Bauer asks Jews: Have you the right from your standpoint to crave political emancipation? we would inquire on the contrary: Has the standpoint of political emancipation the right to demand of Jews the abolition of Judaism, or from men generally the abolition of religion?

The complexion of the Jewish question changes according to the State in which Jews find themselves. In Germany, where no political State, no State as State exists, the Jewish question is a purely theological question. The Jew finds himself in religious antagonism to the State, which acknowledges Christianity as its basis. This State is theologian *ex professo*. Here criticism is criticism of theology, is two-edged criticism, criticism of Christian and criticism of Jewish theology. But however critical we may be, we cannot get out of the theological circle.

In France, in the constitutional State, the Jewish question is the question of constitutionalism, of the incompleteness of political emancipation. As the semblance of a State religion is there preserved, although in a meaningless and self-contradictory formula, in the formula of a religion of the majority, the relationship of Jews to the State retains the semblance of a religious and theological antagonism.

It is only in the North American Free States—at least in part of them—that the Jewish question loses its theological significance and becomes a really secular question. Only where the political State exists in its completeness can the relation of the

Jew, of the religious man generally, to the political State, and therefore the relation of religion to the State, be studied in its special features and its purity. The criticism of this relationship ceases to be theological criticism when the State ceases to adopt a theological attitude towards religion, when its attitude towards religion becomes purely political. The criticism then becomes criticism of the political State. At this point, where the question ceases to be theological, Bauer's criticism ceases to be critical. In the United States there is neither a State religion nor a religion declared to be that of the majority, nor the predominance of one cult over another. The State is alien to all cults. (*Marie ou l'esclavage aux Etats-Unis*, etc., by G. Beaumont, Paris 1835, p. 214.) There are even North American States where "the constitution does not impose religious beliefs or the practice of a cult as a condition of political privileges" (l. c. p. 225). Yet "nobody in the United States believes that a man without religion might be an honest man" (l. c. p. 224). Yet North America is pre-eminently the country of religiosity, as Beaumont, Tocqueville and the Englishman Hamilton assure us with one voice. Meanwhile, the North American States only serve us as an example. The question is: What is the attitude of completed political emancipation towards religion? If even in the country of completed political emancipation we find religion not only existing, but in a fresh and vital state, it proves that the existence of religion does not contradict the completeness of the State. But as the existence of religion indicates the presence of a defect, the source of this defect may only be looked for in the nature of the State. We are no longer concerned with religion as the basis, but only as the phenomenon of secular shortcomings. Consequently we explain the religious handicap of the free citizens from their secular handicap. We do not assert that they must remove their religious handicap as soon as they cast off their secular fetters. We do not transform secular questions into theological questions. We transform theological questions into secular questions.

After history has for so long been dissolved in superstition, we dissolve the superstition in history. The question of the relation of political emancipation becomes for us the question of the relation of political emancipation to human emancipation. We criticize the religious weakness of the political State by criticizing the political State in its secular construction, apart from the religious weaknesses. We transmute the contradiction of the State with a specific religion, like Judaism, into the contradiction of the State with specific secular elements, and the contradiction of the State with religion generally into the contradiction of the State with its general assumptions.

The political emancipation of the Jew, of the Christian, of the religious man in general, means the emancipation of the State from Judaism, from Christianity, from religion generally. In its form as State, in the manner peculiar to its nature, the State emancipates itself from religion by emancipating itself from the State religion, that is, by the State as State acknowledging no religion.

Political emancipation from religion is not a thorough-going and consistent emancipation from religion, because political emancipation is not effectual and consistent human emancipation.

The limit of political emancipation is immediately seen to consist in the fact that the State can cast off a fetter without men really becoming free from it, that the State can become a free State without men becoming free men. Bauer tacitly assents to this in laying down the following condition for political emancipation. "Every religious privilege, and therefore the monopoly of a privileged Church must be surrendered, and if few or many or even the great majority believe they ought still to perform religious duties, this performance must be left to themselves as a private matter." The State may therefore achieve emancipation from religion, although the great majority are still religious. And the great majority do not cease to be religious by being religious privately.

The political elevation of the individual above religion shares all the defects and all the advantages of political elevation generally. For example, the State as State annuls private property, the individual declares in a political manner that private property is abolished as soon as he abolishes the census for active and passive eligibility, which has been done in many North American States. Hamilton interprets this fact quite correctly from the political standpoint: "The great multitude has won the victory over the property owners and the monied men." Is not private property ideally abolished when the have-nots become the legislators of the haves? The census is the last political form to recognize private property.

Yet private property is not only not abolished with the political annulment of private property, but is even implied therein. The State abolishes in its fashion the distinctions of birth, status, education, and occupation when it declares birth, status, education, and occupation to be unpolitical distinctions, when, without taking account of these distinctions, it calls upon every member of the community to participate in the popular sovereignty on an equal footing, when it deals with all the elements of the real popular life from the State's point of view. Nevertheless the State leaves private property, education, occupation operating in their own manner, that is, as education, as occupation, and developing their potentialities.

From abolishing these actual distinctions, it rather exists only upon their basis, and is conscious of being a political State and enforcing its communal principle only in opposition to these its elements. Consequently Hegel defines the relation of the political State to religion quite correctly when he says: "If the State is to have reality as the ethical, self-conscious realization of spirit, it must be distinguished from the form of authority and faith. But this distinction arises only in so far as the ecclesiastical side is in itself divided into several churches. Then only is the State seen to be superior to them, and wins and brings into existence the universality of thought as the principle of its form." ("Philosophy of Right," Eng. tr. p. 270.)

By its nature the completed political State is the generic life of man in contradistinction to his material life. All the assumptions of this egoistic life remain in existence outside the sphere of the State, in bourgeois society, but as the peculiarities of bourgeois society.

Where the political State has attained its true development, the individual leads not only in thought, in consciousness, but in reality, a double life, a heavenly and an earthly life, a life in the political community, wherein he counts as a member of the community, and a life in bourgeois society, wherein he is active as a private person, regarding other men as a means, degrading himself into a means and becoming a plaything of alien powers.

The political State is related to bourgeois society as spiritualistically as heaven is to earth. It occupies the same position of antagonism towards bourgeois society; it subdues the latter just as religion overcomes the limitations of the profane world, that is, by recognizing bourgeois society and allowing the latter to dominate it. Man in his outermost reality, in bourgeois society, is a profane being. Here, where he is a real individual for himself and others, he is an untrue phenomenon.

In the State, on the other hand, where the individual is a generic being, he is the imaginary member of an imagined sovereignty, he is robbed of his real individual life and filled with an unreal universality.

The conflict in which the individual as the professor of a particular religion is involved with his citizenship, with other individuals as members of the community, reduces itself to the secular cleavage between the political State and bourgeois society.

For the individual as a bourgeois, "life in the State is only a semblance, or a passing exception to the rule and the nature of things." In any case, the bourgeois, like the Jew, remains only sophistically in political life, just as the citizen remains a Jew or a bourgeois only sophistically; but this sophistry is not personal. It is the sophistry of the political State itself. The difference between the religious individual and the citizen is the difference between the merchant and the citizen, between the labourer and the citizen, between the landowner and the citizen, between the living individual and the citizen. The contradiction in which the religious individual is involved with the political individual is the same contradiction in which the bourgeois is involved with the citizen, in which the member of bourgeois society is involved with his political lionskin.

This secular conflict to which the Jewish question is finally reduced, the relation of the political State to its fundamental conditions, whether the latter be material elements, like private property, etc., or spiritual elements, like education or religion, the conflict between the general interest and the private interest, the cleavage between the political State and bourgeois society—these secular antagonisms are left unnoticed by Bauer, while he controverts their religious expression. "It is precisely its foundation, the need which assures to bourgeois society its existence and guarantees its necessity, which exposes its existence to constant dangers, maintains in it an uncertain element and converts the latter into a constantly changing mixture of poverty and wealth, distress and prosperity," p. 8.

Bourgeois society in its antagonism to the political State is recognized as necessary, because the political State is recognized as necessary.

Political emancipation at least represents important progress; while not the last form of human emancipation generally, it is the last form of human emancipation within the existing world order. It is understood that we are speaking here of real, of practical emancipation.

The individual emancipates himself politically from religion by banishing it from public right into private right. It is no longer the spirit of the State, where the individual—although in a limited manner, under a particular form and in a special sphere—behaves as a generic being, in conjunction with other individuals; it has become the spirit of bourgeois society, of the sphere of egoism, of the *bellum omnium contra omnes*.[6] It is no longer the essence of the community, but the essence of social distinctions.

It has become the expression of the separation of the individual from his community, from himself and from other

6   The war of all against all.

individuals—what it was originally. It is only the abstract profession of special perversity, of private whim. The infinite splitting-up of religion in North America, for example, gives it outwardly the form of a purely individual concern. It has been added to the heap of private interests, and exiled from the community as community. But there is no misunderstanding about the limits of political emancipation. The division of the individual into a public and a private individual, the expulsion of religion from the State into bourgeois society, is not a step, it is the completion of political emancipation, which thus neither abolishes nor seeks to abolish the real religiosity of the individual.

The splitting-up of the individual into Jew and citizen, into Protestant and citizen, into a religious person and citizen, this decomposition does not belie citizenship; it is not a circumvention of political emancipation; it is political emancipation itself, it is the political manner of becoming emancipated from religion. Moreover, in times when the political State as a political State is forcibly born of bourgeois society, when human self-liberation strives to realize itself under the form of political self-liberation, the State is driven the whole length of abolishing, of destroying religion, but it also proceeds to the abolition of private property, to the law of maximum, to confiscation, to progressive taxation, just as it proceeds to the abolition of life, to the guillotine. In the moment of its heightened consciousness, the political life seeks to suppress its fundamental conditions, bourgeois society and its elements, and to constitute itself as the real and uncontradictory generic life of the individual. It is, however, only enabled to do this by a flagrant violation of its own conditions of life, by declaring the revolution to be permanent, and the political drama therefore ends as inevitably with the restoration of religion, of private property, and all the elements of bourgeois society, as war ends with peace.

Why not even the so-called Christian State, which acknowledges Christianity as its basis, as the State religion, and therefore adopts a proscriptive attitude towards other religions is the completed Christian State. The latter is rather

the atheistic State, the democratic State, the State which con-
signs religion among the other elements of bourgeois society.
The State which is still theological and which still officially
prescribes belief in Christianity, has not yet succeeded in
giving secular and human expression to those human foundations whose exaggerated expression is Christianity. The
so-called Christian State is simply no State at all, because
it is not Christianity as a religion, but only the human back-
ground of the Christian religion which can realize itself in
actual human creations.

The so-called Christian State is the Christian denial of the
State, although it is not by any means the political realization
of Christianity. The State, which still professes Christianity in
the form of religion, does not yet profess it in the form of the
State, for its attitude towards religion is a religious attitude. It
is not yet the actual realization of the human basis of religion,
because it still operates upon the unreality, upon the imaginary shape of this human kernel. The so-called Christian State
is the incomplete State, and the Christian religion is regarded
by it as the complement and the redemption of its imperfection. Consequently religion becomes its instrument, and it is
the State of hypocrisy. The so-called Christian State needs the
Christian religion in order to complete itself as a State. The
democratic State, the real State, does not need religion for its
political completion. It can rather do without religion, because
it represents the realization of the human basis of religion in
a secular manner. The so-called Christian State, on the other
hand, adopts a political attitude towards religion and a religious attitude towards politics. If it degrades the State form to
the level of a fiction, it equally degrades religion to a fiction.

In order to elucidate these antagonisms, let us consider Bauer's
construction of the Christian State, a construction which has
proceeded from contemplating the Christian-Germanic State.

Says Bauer: "In order to demonstrate the impossibility or the
non-existence of a Christian State, we are frequently referred
to that pronouncement in the Gospel which it not only does
not follow, but cannot follow without dissolving itself com-

pletely as a State." "But the question is not settled so easily. What then does this Gospel text enjoin? Supernatural self-denial, subjection to the authority of revelation, the turning away from the State, the abolition of secular conditions. Now all this is enjoined and carried out by the Christian State. It has absorbed the spirit of the Gospel, and if it does not repeat it in the same words as the Gospel expresses it, the reason is only because it expresses this spirit in the State form, that is, in forms which are indeed derived from the State of this world, but which are degraded to a sham in the religious rebirth which they have to undergo."

Bauer goes on to show how the people of the Christian State are only a sham people, who no longer have any will of their own, but possess their real existence in the chief to whom they are subject, but from whom they were originally and naturally alien, as he was given to them by God; how the laws of this people are not their creation, but positive revelations; how their chief requires privileged mediators with his own people, with the masses; how these masses themselves are split up into a multitude of special circles, which are formed and determined by chance, which are distinguished by their interests, their particular passions and prejudices, and receive as a privilege permission to make mutual compacts (p. 56).

The separation of the "spirit of the Gospel" from the "letter of the Gospel" is an irreligious act. The State, which makes the Gospel speak in the letter of politics, in other letters than those of the Holy Spirit, commits a sacrilege if not in human eyes, at least in its own religious eyes. The State, which acknowledges Christianity as its supreme embodiment and the Bible as its charter, must be confronted with the words of Holy Writ, for the writings are sacred to the letter. The State lapses into a painful, and from the standpoint of the religious consciousness, irresolvable contradiction, when it is pinned down to that pronouncement of the Gospel, which it "not only does not follow, but cannot follow without completely dissolving itself as a State." And why does it not want to completely dissolve itself? To this question it can find no answer, either for itself or for others. In its own consciousness the official Christian State is an Ought, which is impossible of realization. Only by lies can it persuade itself of the reality of its existence, and consequently it always remains for itself an object of doubt, an unreliable and ambiguous object. The critic is therefore quite justified in forcing the State, which appeals to the Bible, into a condition of mental derangement where it no longer knows whether it is a phantasm or a reality, where the infamy of its secular objects, for which religion serves as a mantle, falls into irresolvable conflict with the integrity of its religious consciousness, to which religion appears as the object of the world. This State can only redeem itself from its inner torment by becoming the hangman of the Catholic Church. As against the latter, which declares the secular power to be its serving body, the State is impotent. Impotent is the secular power which claimed to be the rule of the religious spirit.

In the so-called Christian State it is true that alienation counts, but not the individual. The only individual who counts, the king, is a being specially distinguished from other individuals, who is also religious and directly connected with heaven, with God. The relations which here prevail are still relations of faith. The religious spirit is therefore not yet really secularized.

Moreover, the religious spirit cannot be really secularized, for what in fact is it but the unworldly form of a stage in the development of the human mind? The religious spirit can only be realized in so far as the stage of development of the human mind, whose religious expression it is, emerges and constitutes itself in its secular form. This is what happens in the democratic State. It is not Christianity, but the human basis of Christianity which is the basis of this State. Religion remains the ideal, unworldly consciousness of its members, because it is the ideal form of the human stage of development which it represents.

The members of the political State are religious by virtue of the dualism between the individual life and the generic life, between the life of bourgeois society and the political life; they are religious inasmuch as the individual regards as his true life the political life beyond his real individuality, in so far as religion is here the spirit of bourgeois society, the expression of the separation and the alienation of man from man. The political democracy is Christian to the extent that it regards every individual as the sovereign, the supreme being, but it means the individual in his uncultivated, unsocial aspect, the individual in his fortuitous existence, the individual just as he is, the individual as he is destroyed, lost, and alienated through the whole organization of our society, as he is given under the dominance of inhuman conditions and elements, in a word, the individual who is not yet a real generic being.

The sovereignty of the individual, as an alien being distinguished from the real individual, which is the chimera, the dream, and the postulate of Christianity, is under democracy sensual reality, the present, and the secular maximum.

The religious and theological consciousness itself is heightened and accentuated under a completed democracy, because it is apparently without political significance, without earthly aims, an affair of misanthropic feeling, the expression of narrow-mindedness, the product of caprice, because it is a really other-worldly life. Here Christianity achieves the practical expression of its universal religious significance, in that the most various philosophies are marshalled in the form of Christianity, and, what is more, other members of society are not required to subscribe to Christianity, but to some kind of religion. The religious consciousness riots in the wealth of religious antagonism and of religious variety.

We have therefore shown: Political emancipation from religion leaves religion in existence, although not as a privileged religion. The contradiction in which the supporter of a particular religion finds himself involved with his citizenship, is only a part of the general secular contradiction between the political State and bourgeois society. The completion of the Christian State is the State which professes to be a State and abstracts from the religion of its members. The emancipation of the State from religion is not the emancipation of the real individual from religion.

We do not therefore tell the Jews with Bauer: You cannot be politically emancipated without radically emancipating your-selves from Judaism. We tell them rather: Because you could be emancipated politically without entirely breaking away from Judaism, political emancipation is not human emancipa-tion. If you Jews desire to be politically emancipated without emancipating yourselves humanly, the incompleteness, the contradiction, lies not only in you, but it also resides in the es-sence and the category of political emancipation. If you remain enmeshed in this category, you share in a general disability.

But if the individual, although a Jew, can be politically emanci-pated and receive civic rights, can he claim and receive the so-called rights of man? Bauer denies it: "The question is whether the Jew as such, that is the Jew who admits that by his very nature he is compelled to live in everlasting separation from others, is capable of receiving and conceding to others the gen-eral rights of man."

"The idea of the rights of man was first discovered in the last century so far as the Christian world is concerned. It is not in-nate in the individual, it is rather conquered in the struggle with the historical traditions in which the individual has hith-erto been brought up. Thus the rights of man are not a gift from Nature, not a legacy from past history, but the price of the struggle against the accident of birth and against the privileges which history has bequeathed from generation to generation up to now. They are the result of education, and can only be possessed by those who have acquired and earned them."

"Can they really be claimed by the Jew? So long as he is a Jew, the limiting quality which makes him a Jew must triumph over the human quality which binds him as a man to other men, and must separate him from gentiles. By this separa-tion he proclaims that the special quality which makes him a Jew is his real supreme quality, to which the human quality must give place."

"In the same manner the Christian as Christian cannot grant the rights of man," pp. 19, 20.

According to Bauer, the individual must sacrifice the "privilege of faith" in order to be able to receive the general rights of man. Let us consider for a moment the so-called rights of man, in fact the rights of man in their authentic shape, in the shape which they possess among their discoverers, the North Americans and the French. In part these rights of man are political rights, rights which are only exercised in the community with others. Participation in the affairs of the community, in fact of the political community, forms their substance. They come within the category of political freedom, of civil rights, which does not, as we have seen, by any means presuppose the unequivocal and positive abolition of religion, and therefore of Judaism. It remains to consider the other aspect of human rights, the *droits de l'homme* apart from the *droits du citoyen*.

Among them is to be found liberty of conscience, the right to practise any cult to one's liking. The privilege of belief is expressly recognized, either as a human right or as the consequence of a human right, of freedom.

Declaration of the rights of man and of citizenship, 1791, article 10:[7] *No penalty should attach to the holding of religious opinions. The right of every man to practise the religious cult to which he is attached is guaranteed by clause 1 of the Constitution of 1791.*

The Declaration of the Rights of Man, etc., 1793, includes among human rights, article 7: The free practice of cults. With respect to the right to publish ideas and opinions and to assemble for the practice of a cult, it is even stated: The necessity for enunciating these rights presupposes either the presence or the recent memory of a despotism.

Constitution of Pennsylvania, article 9, paragraph 3: All men have received from Nature the imprescriptible right to worship the Almighty according to the dictates of their conscience, and nobody may legally be constrained to follow, to institute, or to support, against his will, any religious cult or ministry.

---

7   The italicized passages following are given in French in the original.

43

In no case may any human authority interfere in questions of conscience and control the prerogatives of the soul.

Constitution of New Hampshire, articles 5 and 6: Among the number of natural rights, some are inalienable by their nature, because nothing can take their place. Such are the rights of conscience.

The incompatibility of religion with the rights of man is thus not implied by the conception of the rights of man, because the right to be religious, to be religious according to one's liking, to practise the cult of a particular religion, is expressly included among the rights of man. The privilege of faith is a general right of man.

The rights of man as such are distinguished from the rights of the citizen. What is man apart from the citizen? Nothing else than a member of bourgeois society. Why is the member of bourgeois society called "man," and why are his rights called the rights of man? How do we explain this fact? From the relation of the political State to bourgeois society, from the meaning of political emancipation.

Above all we must record the fact that the so-called rights of man, as distinguished from the rights of the citizen, are nothing else than the rights of the member of bourgeois society, that is of the egoistic individual, of man separated from man and the community. The most radical constitution, the Constitution of 1793, may be cited:

Declaration of the rights of man and of the citizen. Article 2. These rights, etc. (natural and imprescriptible rights) are: equality, liberty, security, property.

Of what consists liberty? *Article 6. Liberty is the power which belongs to man to do everything which does not injure the rights of others.*

Freedom is therefore the right to do and perform that which injures none. The limits within which each may move without injuring others are fixed by the law, as the boundary between two fields is fixed by the fence. The freedom in question is the freedom of the individual as an isolated atom thrown back upon itself. Why, according to Bauer, is the Jew incapable of receiving the rights of man? "So long as he is a Jew, the limiting quality which makes him a Jew must triumph over the human quality which binds him as a man to other men, and must separate him from gentiles." But the right of man to freedom is not based upon the connection of man with man, but rather on the separation of man from man. It is the right to this separation, the right of the individual limited to himself.

The practical application of the right of man to freedom is the right of man to private property.

In what consists the right of man to private property?

Article 16 (Const. of 1793): The right to property is the right of every citizen to enjoy and dispose of as he likes his goods, his income, the fruit of his toil and of his industry.

The right of man to private property is therefore the right to enjoy and dispose of his property, at his will and pleasure, without regard for others, and independently of society: the right of self-interest. Each particular individual freedom exercised in this way forms the basis of bourgeois society. It leaves every man to find in other men not the realization, but rather the limits of his freedom. But it proclaims above all the right of man to enjoy and dispose of his property, his income, and the fruit of his toil and his industry according to his pleasure.

There still remain the other rights of man, equality and security.

Equality here in its non-political significance is nothing but the equality of the above described liberty, viz.: every individual is regarded as a uniform atom resting on its own bottom. Article 5 of the *Constitution of 1793* states: *Equality consists in the fact that the law is the same for all, whether it protects or whether it punishes.*

And security? *Article 8 of the Constitution of 1793: Security consists in the protection accorded by society to each of its members for the preservation of his person, his rights, and his property.*

Security is the supreme social conception of bourgeois society, the conception of the police, the idea that society as a whole only exists to guarantee to each of its members the maintenance of his person, his rights, and his property.

By the conception of security bourgeois society does not raise itself above its egoism. Security is rather the confirmation of its egoism.

None of the so-called rights of man, therefore, goes beyond the egoistic individual, beyond the individual as a member of bourgeois society, withdrawn into his private interests and separated from the community. Far from regarding the individual as a generic being, the generic life, Society itself, rather appears as an external frame for the individual, as a limitation of his original independence. The sole bond which connects him with his fellows is natural necessity, material needs and private interest, the preservation of his property and his egoistic person.

It is strange that a people who were just beginning to free themselves, to break down all the barriers between the various members of the community, to establish a political community, that such a people should solemnly proclaim the justification of the egoistic individual, separated from his fellows and from the community, and should even repeat this declaration at a moment when the most heroic sacrifice could alone save the nation and was therefore urgently required, at a moment when the sacrifice of all interests of bourgeois society was imperative, and egoism should have been punished as a crime. This fact is even stranger when we behold the political liberators degrading citizenship and the political community to the level of a mere means for the maintenance of these so-called rights of man, proclaiming the citizen to be the servant of the egoistic man, degrading the sphere in which the individual behaves as a social being below the sphere in which he behaves as a fractional being, and finally accepting as the true proper man not the individual as citizen, but the individual as bourgeois.

The aim of every political association is the preservation of the natural and imprescriptible rights of man. (Declaration of the rights, etc., of 1791, article 2.) The purpose of government is to assure to man the enjoyment of his natural and imprescriptible rights. (Declaration of 1793, art. 1.)

Thus even at the time when its enthusiasm was still fresh and kept at boiling point by the pressure of circumstances, the political life proclaimed itself to be a mere means whose end is the life of bourgeois society.

It is true that its revolutionary practice was in flagrant contradiction to its theory. While security, for example, was proclaimed to be a right of man, the violation of the secrecy of correspondence was publicly proposed.

While the indefinite liberty of the press (1793 Constitution, art. 122) was guaranteed as a consequence of the right of man to individual liberty, the freedom of the press was completely destroyed, for liberty of the press could not be permitted when it compromised public liberty. (Robespierre jeune, "Parliamentary History of the French Revolution." Buchez et Roux, p. 135.) This means that the right of man to liberty ceases to be a right as soon as it comes into conflict with the political life, whereas, according to theory, the political life is only the guarantee of the rights of man, and should therefore be surrendered as soon as its object contradicts these rights of man. But the practice is only the exception and the theory is the rule. If, however, we regard the revolutionary practice as the correct position of the relation, the riddle still remains to be solved, why the relationship was inverted in the consciousness of the political liberators, the end appearing as the means, and the means as the end. This optical illusion of their consciousness would still be the same riddle, although a psychological, a theoretical riddle.

The riddle admits of easy solution.

47

The political emancipation is at the same time the dissolution of the old society, upon which was based the civic society, or the rulership alienated from the people. The political
revolution is the revolution of bourgeois society. What was the
character of the old society? It can be described in one word.
Feudality. The old civic society had a directly political character, that is, the elements of civic life, as for example property
or the family, or the mode and kind of labour, were raised to
the level of elements of the community in the form of landlord-
ism, status, and corporation. In this form they determined the
relation of the individual to the community, that is his political
relation, his relationship of separation and exclusion from the
other constituent parts of society. For the latter organization
of popular life did not raise property or labour to the level of
social elements, but rather completed their separation from
the political whole and constituted them as special societies
within society. Thus the vital functions and vital conditions
of society continued to be political, although political in the
sense of feudality, which means that they excluded the individual from the political whole, and transformed the special
relation of his corporation to the political whole into his own
general relation to the popular life. As a consequence of this
organization, the political unity necessarily appears as the
consciousness, the will and the activity of the political unity,
and likewise the general State power as the special concern of
a ruler and his servants sundered from the people.

The political revolution, which overthrew this domination and
raised political affairs to the rank of popular affairs, which
constituted the political State as a general concern, that is as
a real State, necessarily shattered all Estates, corporations,
guilds, privileges, which were just so many expressions of
the separation of the people from their community. The political revolution thereby abolished the political character of
civic society.

It dissolved civic society into its elemental parts, on the one
hand, into the individuals, on the other hand, into the material
and spiritual elements, which formed the vital content, the civic situation of these individuals. It released the political spirit,

which was imprisoned in fragments in the various blind alleys of the feudal society; it collected all these dispersed parts of it, liberated it from its entanglement with the civic life, and constituted it as the sphere of the community, of the general popular concerns in ideal independence from its particular elements of civic life. The specific life activity and the specific life situation settled into a merely general significance. They no longer formed the general relation of the individual to the political whole. The public business as such became rather the general business of every individual and the political function became his general function.

But the completion of the idealism of the State was at the same time the completion of the materialism of civic society.

The throwing off of the political yoke was at the same time the throwing off of the bond which had curbed the egoistic spirit of civic society. The political emancipation was at the same time the emancipation of civic society from politics, from even the semblance of a general content.

Feudal society was resolved into its basic elements, its individual members. But into the individuals who really formed its basis, that is, the egoistic individual.

This individual, the member of civic society, is now the basis, the assumption of the political State. He is recognized as such in the rights of man.

The liberty of the egoistic individual and the recognition of this liberty are, however, tantamount to the recognition of the unbridled movement of the intellectual and material elements which inform him.

The individual was therefore not liberated from religion; he received religious freedom. He was not freed from property; he received freedom of property. He was not freed from the egoism of industry; he received industrial freedom.

The constitution of the political State and the dissolution of civic society into independent individuals—whose relation is right, as the relation of the members of Estates and of guilds was privilege—is accomplished in one and the same act. But the individual as a member of civic society, the unpolitical individual, necessarily appears as the natural individual. The rights of man appear as natural rights, for the self-conscious activity concentrates itself upon the political act. The egoistic individual is the sediment of the dissolved society, the object of immediate certitude, and therefore a natural object. The political revolution dissolves the civic society into its constituent parts without revolutionizing and subjecting to criticism those parts themselves. It regards bourgeois society, the world of needs, of labour, of private interests, as the foundation of its existence, as an assumption needing no proof, and therefore as its natural basis. Lastly, the individual as a member of bourgeois society counts as the proper individual, as the man in contradistinction to the citizen, because he is man in his sensual, individual, closest existence, whereas political man is only the abstract, artificial individual, the individual as an allegorical, moral person. The real man is only recognized in the shape of the egoistic individual, the true man is only recognized in the shape of the abstract citizen.

The abstraction of the political man was very well described by Rousseau: *He who dares undertake to give instructions to a nation ought to feel himself capable as it were of changing human nature; of transforming every individual who in himself is a complete and independent whole into part of a greater whole, from which he receives in some manner his life and his being; of altering man's constitution, in order to strengthen it; of substituting a social and moral existence for the independent and physical existence which we have all received from nature. In a word, it is necessary to deprive man of his native powers, in order to endow him with some which are alien to him, and of which he cannot make use without the aid of other people.*

All emancipation leads back to the human world, to relationships, to men themselves.

Political emancipation is the reduction of man, on the one side, to the member of bourgeois society, to the egoistic, independent individual, on the other side, to the citizen, to the moral person.

Not until the real, individual man is identical with the citizen, and has become a generic being in his empirical life, in his individual work, in his individual relationships, not until man has recognized and organized his own capacities as social capacities, and consequently the social force is no longer divided by the political power, not until then will human emancipation be achieved.

2. *The Capacity of Modern Jews and Christians to become Free,* by BRUNO BAUER.

Under this form Bauer deals with the relation of the Jewish and Christian religion, as well as with the relation of the same to criticism. Its relation to criticism is its relation "to the capacity to be free."

It follows: "The Christian has only one stage to surmount, viz.: his religion, in order to abolish religion generally," and therefore to become free. "The Jew, on the contrary, has to break not only with his Jewish essence, but also with the development of the completion of his religion, with a development that has remained alien to him" (p. 71).

Bauer therefore transforms here the question of Jewish emancipation into a purely religious question. The theological scruple as to who stood the most chance of being saved, Jew or Christian, is here repeated in the enlightened form: which of the two is most capable of emancipation? It is no longer a question of whether Judaism or Christianity makes free? but rather on the contrary: which makes more for freedom, the negation of Judaism or the negation of Christianity?

"If they wish to be free, Jews should be converted, not to Christianity, but to Christianity in dissolution, to religion generally in dissolution, that is to enlightenment, criticism and its results, to free humanity," p. 70.

It appears that Jews have still to be converted, but to Christianity in dissolution, instead of to Christianity.

Bauer requires Jews to break with the essence of the Christian religion, a requirement which, as he says himself, does not arise from the development of Jewish essentials.

As Bauer had interpreted Judaism merely as a crude-religious criticism of Christianity, and had therefore read "only" a religious meaning into it, it was to be foreseen that the emancipation of the Jews would be transformed into a philosophic-theological act.

Bauer conceives the ideal abstract being of the Jew, his religion as his whole being. Consequently he correctly infers: "The Jew gives mankind nothing, when he despises his narrow law, when he abolishes his whole Judaism," p. 65.

The relation of Jews and Christians is therefore as follows: the sole interest of Christians in the emancipation of the Jews is a general human, a theoretical interest. Judaism is a detrimental fact in the religious eyes of Christians. As soon as their eyes cease to be religious, this fact ceases to be detrimental. The emancipation of Jews in itself is no work for Christians.

But in order to emancipate himself, the Jew has to undertake not only his own work, but at the same time the work of the Christian, the criticism of the synoptics, etc.

We will try to get rid of the theological conception of the question. The question of the capacity of the Jews for emancipation is from our standpoint transformed into the question, what particular social element has to be overcome in order to abolish Judaism? For the capacity for emancipation of the modern Jew is the relation of Judaism to the emancipation of the modern world. This relation is necessarily disclosed by the special position of Judaism in the modern subjugated world.

Let us consider the real worldly Jews, not the Sabbath Jews, as Bauer does, but the every-day Jews.

We will not look for the secret of the Jew in his religion, but we will look for the secret of religion in the real Jew.

What is the secular basis of Judaism? Practical needs, egoism.

What is the secular cult of the Jew? Huckstering. What is his secular God? Money.

Very well. Emancipation from huckstering and from money, and therefore from practical, real Judaism would be the self-emancipation of our epoch.

An organization of society, which would abolish the fundamental conditions of huckstering, and therefore the possibility of huckstering, would render the Jew impossible. His religious consciousness would dissolve like a mist in the real vital air of society. On the other hand: if the Jew recognizes as valueless this his practical essence, and labours for its abolition, he would work himself free of his previous development, and labour for human emancipation generally, turning against the supreme practical expression of human self-alienation.

We therefore perceive in Judaism a general pervading anti-social element, which has been carried to its highest point by the historical development, in which Jews in this bad relation have zealously co-operated, a point at which it must necessarily dissolve itself.

The emancipation of the Jews in its last significance is the emancipation of mankind from Judaism.

The Jew has already emancipated himself in Jewish fashion. "The Jew who in Vienna, for example, is only tolerated, determines by his financial power the fate of the whole Empire. The Jew who may be deprived of rights in the smallest German State, determines the fate of Europe."

"While the corporations and guilds excluded the Jew, the enterprise of industry laughs at the obstinacy of the medieval institution." (Bauer, "The Jewish Question," p. 14.)

This is no isolated fact. The Jew has emancipated himself in Jewish fashion, not only by taking to himself financial power, but by virtue of the fact that with and without his co-operation, money has become a world power, and the practical Jewish spirit has become the practical spirit of Christian nations. The Jews have emancipated themselves in so far as Christians have become Jews.

"The pious and politically free inhabitant of New England," relates Colonel Hamilton, "is a kind of Laokoon, who does not make even the slightest effort to free himself from the serpents which are throttling him. Mammon is his god, he prays to him, not merely with his lips, but with all the force of his body and mind.

"In his eyes, the world is nothing more than a Stock Exchange, and he is convinced that here below he has no other destiny than to become richer than his neighbours. When he travels, he carries his shop or his counter on his back, so to speak, and talks of nothing but interest and profit."

The practical domination of Judaism over the Christian world has reached such a point in North America that the preaching of the Gospel itself, the Christian ministry, has become an article of commerce, and the bankrupt merchant takes to the Gospel, while the minister grown rich goes into business.

"He whom you see at the head of a respectable congregation began as a merchant; his business failing, he became a minister. The other started his career in the ministry, but as soon as he had saved a sum of money, he abandoned the pulpit for the counter. In the eyes of a large number, the ministry is a commercial career." Beaumont.

According to Bauer, to withhold political rights from the Jew in theory, while in practice he wields enormous power, exercising wholesale the influence he is forbidden to distribute in retail, is an anomaly.

The contradiction between the practical, political power of the Jew and his political rights is the contradiction between politics and financial power generally. While the former is raised ideally above the latter, it has in reality become its bond slave.

Judaism has persisted alongside of Christianity not only as religious criticism of Christianity, not only as the embodiment of doubt in the religious parentage of Christianity, but equally because Judaism has maintained itself, and even received its supreme development, in Christian society. The Jew who exists as a peculiar member of bourgeois society, is only the particular expression of the Judaism of bourgeois society.

Judaism has survived not in spite of, but by virtue of history.

Out of its own entrails, bourgeois society continually creates Jews.

What was the foundation of the Jewish religion? Practical needs, egoism. Consequently the monotheism of the Jew is in reality the polytheism of many needs. Practical needs or egoism are the principle of bourgeois society, and they appear openly as such so soon as bourgeois society gives birth to the political state. The God of practical needs and egoism is money.

Money is the jealous God of Israel, by the side of which no other god may exist. Money degrades all the gods of man and converts them into commodities. Money is the general and self-constituted value of all things. Consequently it has robbed the whole world—the world of mankind as well as Nature—of its peculiar value. Money is the being of man's work and existence alienated from himself, and this alien being rules him, and he prays to it.

The God of the Jews has secularized himself and become the universal God. Exchange is the Jew's real God.

The conception of Nature which prevails under the rule of private property and of money is the practical degradation of Nature, which indeed exists in the Jewish religion, but only in imagination.

In this sense Thomas Muenzer declared it to be intolerable "that all creatures have been turned into property, the fishes in the water, the birds in the air, the growths of the soil."

What remains as the abstract part of the Jewish religion, contempt for theory, for art, for history, for man as an end in himself, is the real conscious standpoint and virtue of the monied man. The generic relation itself—the relation of man to woman, etc., becomes an object of commerce. Woman is bartered.

The chimerical nationality of the Jew is the nationality of the merchant, of the monied man generally.

The baseless law of the Jew is only the religious caricature of the baseless morality and of right generally, of the merely formal ceremonies which pervade the world of egoism.

Here also the highest relation of man is the legal relation—the relation to laws which do not govern him because they are the laws of his own will and being, but because they are imposed on him from without. Any infraction thereof is punished.

Jewish Jesuitism, the same practical Jesuitism that Bauer infers from the Talmud, is the relation of the world of egoism to the laws which dominate it, and the cunning circumvention of which is the supreme art of this world.

The movement of this world within its laws is necessarily a continual abrogation of the law.

Judaism cannot develop any further as a religion, that is theoretically, because the philosophy of practical needs is limited by its nature and is exhausted in a few moves.

Judaism could create no new world; it could only draw the new world creations and world relations within the orbit of its activity, because the practical need whose rationale is egoism remains a passive state, which does not extend itself by spontaneous act, but only expands with the development of social conditions.

Judaism reaches its acme with the completion of bourgeois society, but bourgeois society first completes itself in the Christian world. Only under the reign of Christianity, which turns all national, natural, moral and theoretical relations into relations external to man, can bourgeois society separate itself entirely from the political life, dissever all the generic ties of the individual, set egoism in the place of these generic ties, and dissolve the human world into a world of atomized, mutually hostile individuals.

Christianity sprang out of Judaism. It has again withdrawn into Judaism.

The Christian from the outset was the theorizing Jew; the Jew is therefore the practical Christian, and the practical Christian has again become a Jew.

Christianity had only appeared to overcome Judaism. It was too noble, too spiritual to abolish the crudeness of practical needs except by elevation into the blue sky.

Christianity is the sublime idea of Judaism. Judaism is the common application of Christianity, but this application could only become general after Christianity had completed the alienation of man from himself, and theoretically from Nature. Not until then could Judaism attain to general domination and turn the alienated individual and alienated Nature into alienable and saleable objects.

Just as the individual while he remained in the toils of religion could only objectivize his being by turning it into a fantastic and alien being, so under the domination of egoistic needs he can only manifest himself in a practical way and only create practical objects by placing both his products and his activity under the domination of an alien being, and investing them with the significance of an alien being—of money.

The Christian selfishness of bliss is necessarily transmuted in its completed practice into the material selfishness of the Jew, heavenly needs become earthly needs, and subjectivity becomes egoism. We do not explain the Jew's tenacity from his religion, but rather from the human basis of his religion, that is, practical needs, egoism.

Because the real essence of the Jew has been generally realized and secularized in bourgeois society, the latter could not convince the Jew of the unreality of his religious essence, which is merely the ideal reflexion of his practical needs.

Consequently, it is not only in the Pentateuch or the Talmud, but also in present-day society that we find the essence of the modern Jew; not as an abstract, but as an extremely empirical being, not merely in the form of the Jew's limitations, but in that of the Jewish limitations of society.

As soon as society succeeds in abolishing the empirical essence of Judaism, the huckster, and the conditions which produce him, the Jew will become impossible, because his consciousness will no longer have a corresponding object, because the subjective basis of Judaism, viz.: practical needs, will have been humanized, because the conflict of the individual sensual existence with the generic existence of the individual will have been abolished.

The social emancipation of the Jew is the emancipation of society from Judaism.

ON THE KING OF PRUSSIA AND SOCIAL REFORM

No. 60 of "Vorwaerts" contained an article entitled "The King of Prussia and Social Reform," signed "A Prussian."[8]

In the first place, the so-called Prussian refers to the contents of the Royal Prussian Cabinet Order touching the Silesian weavers' revolt and the opinion of the French journal *La Reforme* upon the Prussian Cabinet Order. *La Reforme* considers that "the fears and the religious feeling of the King" are the source of the Cabinet Order. It even finds in this document a foreshadowing of the great reforms which are in prospect for bourgeois society. "Prussian" instructs *La Reforme* as follows:

> "The King and German society have not reached the stage of foreshadowing their reform, and even the Silesian and Bohemian revolts have not created this state of mind. It is impossible to regard the partial distress of the factory districts as a general question for an unpolitical country like Germany, let alone as a blot upon the whole civilized world. For the Germans the incident has the same significance as any local drought or famine. Consequently the King regards it in the light of a defect of administration or a lack of charity. For the same reason, and because a few soldiers settled accounts with the weak weavers, the destruction of factories and machines caused no fears to the King and the authorities. Even religious feeling did not dictate the Cabinet Order, which is a very sober expression of Chris-

---

8   Arnold Ruge was the author of this article.

tian statecraft, and a doctrine which puts no obstacle in the way of the acceptance of its medicine: the good feeling of Christian hearts. Poverty and crime are two great evils; who can remedy them? The State and the authorities? No, but the union of all Christian hearts."

The so-called Prussian denies the existence of the King's "fears" on the ground, amongst others, that a few soldiers settled accounts with the weak weavers.

In a country then where festivals accompanied by liberal toasts and liberal champagne froth—the Dusseldorf festival will be recalled in this connection—provoke a Royal Cabinet Order, not a single soldier being required, for the purpose of crushing the longing of the whole liberal bourgeoisie for the freedom of the Press and a constitution; in a country where passive obedience is the order of the day; in such a country would the compulsory use of armed force against weak weavers be no event and no startling event? And the weak weavers triumphed at the first encounter. They were suppressed by a subsequently reinforced body of troops. Is the revolt of a crowd of workers less dangerous because it needs no army to suppress it? If the wise Prussian compares the Silesian weavers' revolt with the English labour revolts, the Silesian weavers will appear to him to be strong weavers.

From the general relation of politics to social crime we will explain why the weavers' revolt could cause no special "fears" to the King. For the moment only this need be said: the revolt was directed not immediately against the King of Prussia, but against the bourgeoisie. As an aristocrat and an absolute monarch, the King of Prussia can have no love for the bourgeoisie; he can have even less cause for apprehension when their submission and their impotence are heightened by a strained and difficult relation to the proletariat. Further: the orthodox catholic regards the orthodox protestant with more hostility than the atheist, just as the legitimist regards the liberal with greater hostility than the communist. Not because atheists and communists are related to the catholic and legitimist, but because they are more alien to him than the protestant and the liberal, because they are outside his circle. As a politician, the King of Prussia finds his immediate antagonism in politics, in liberalism.

For the King, the antagonism of the proletariat exists just as little as the King exists for the proletariat. The proletariat must attain to decisive power before it can extinguish antipathies and political antagonisms, and draw upon itself the whole enmity of politics. Lastly: it must even afford a delightful surprise to the well-known character of the King, thirsting for what is interesting and important, to find that "interesting" and "much celebrated" pauperism on his own soil, in conjunction with an opportunity of making people talk about him afresh. How smug he must have felt at the news that henceforth he possessed his "own" Royal Prussian pauperism.

Our "Prussian" is even more unlucky when he denies "religious feeling" to be the source of the Royal Cabinet Order.

Why is not religious feeling the source of this Cabinet Order? Because it is a "very sober" expression of Christian statecraft, a "sober" expression of the doctrine which places no difficulties in the way of the acceptance of its own medicine: the good feeling of Christian hearts.

Is not religious feeling the source of Christian statecraft?

Is not a doctrine which possesses its panacea in the good feeling of Christian hearts based on religious feelings? Does a sober expression of religious feeling cease to be an expression of religious feeling? In fact, it must be a religious feeling greatly infatuated with itself and very intoxicated which would seek in the "unity of Christian hearts the remedy for great evils" which it denies can be supplied by the State and the authorities. It must be a very intoxicated religious feeling which, according to "Prussian's" admission, finds the entire evil to consist in the lack of Christian sentiment, and consequently refers the authorities to the sole means of strengthening this sentiment, to "exhortation." According to "Prussian," Christian feeling is the object at which the Cabinet Order aims. When it is intoxicated, when it is not sober, religious feeling regards itself as the sole good. Where it perceives evil, it ascribes the latter to its own absence, for if it be the only good, it alone can create good.

How then does the so-called Prussian prove that the Cabinet Order is not the outcome of religious feeling? By describing the Cabinet Order everywhere as an outcome of religious feeling. Is an insight into social movements to be expected from such an illogical mind? Listen to his prattle about the relation of German society to the Labour movement and to social reform generally.

Let us distinguish, and this "Prussian" neglects to do, between the various categories that are comprised within the expression "German society": government, bourgeoisie, Press, lastly the workers themselves. These are the various divisions with which we are here concerned. "Prussian" lumps them all together, and appraises them in the lump from a superior standpoint. German society, according to him, has not yet reached the stage of foreshadowing reform.

Why does it lack this instinct?

"In an unpolitical country like Germany," answers "Prussian," "it is impossible to regard the partial distresses of the factory districts as a general question, let alone as a blot on the whole civilized world. The incident has for the Germans the same significance as any local drought or famine. Consequently, the King regards it in the light of a defect in administration or a lack of charity."

"Prussian" therefore explains this inverted conception of labour distress from the peculiarity of an unpolitical country.

It will be conceded that England is a political country. It will be further conceded that England is the country of pauperism, even the word is of English origin.

The study of English conditions is thus the surest means of becoming acquainted with the connection of a political country with pauperism. In England labour distress is not partial but universal, not confined to the factory districts, but co-extensive with the country districts. The movements are not here in their initial stages; they have recurred periodically for almost a century.

Now how does the English bourgeoisie and the government and Press which are connected with it regard pauperism?

So far as the English bourgeoisie places the responsibility for pauperism on politics, the Whig regards the Tory and the Tory the Whig as the cause of pauperism. According to the Whig, the monopoly of large landed property and the prohibitive legislation against the import of corn constitute the chief source of pauperism. According to the Tory, the whole evil is due to Liberalism, to competition, to a factory system that has been carried too far. Neither of the parties finds the cause to reside in politics generally, but each rather in the policy of its opponent; of a reform in society neither party dreams.

The most decisive expression of the English insight into pauperism—we refer always to the insight of the English bourgeoisie and government—is English political economy, that is the scientific reflexion of English economic conditions.

MacCulloch, one of the best and most famous of English political economists, who knows existing conditions and has doubtless a clear insight into the movement of bourgeois society, a pupil of the cynical Ricardo,[9] ventured at a public lecture, amidst applause, to apply to political economy what Bacon said of philosophy: "The man who with true and untiring wisdom suspends his judgment, who progresses gradually, surmounting one after the other the obstacles which impede like mountains the course of study, will in time reach the summit of knowledge, where rest and pure air may be enjoyed, where Nature offers herself to the eye in all her beauty, and whence one may descend by a convenient path to the last details of practice." Good pure air, the pestilential atmosphere of the English cellar dwellings.

---

9   Marx in later years changed his views about MacCulloch and Ricardo.

Great natural beauties, the picturesque rags of the English poor, and the shrivelled flesh of the women, ravaged by work and poverty; children lying in dirt; and the stunted creatures produced by overwork in the one-sided processes of the factories! And the most charming last details of practice: prostitution, murder and the gallows!

Middle class Englishmen who are most alive to the danger of pauperism have an inadequate idea of its causes.

For instance Dr Kay, in his pamphlet *Recent Measures for the Promotion of Education in England*, reduces everything to neglected education. Upon what grounds, think you? Owing to the lack of education, the worker fails to perceive the "natural laws of trade," laws which necessarily bring him to pauperism. Consequently he is up in arms against them. This is calculated to "disturb the prosperity of English manufactures and of English trade, destroy the mutual confidence of business people, weaken the stability of political and social institutions."

So great is the thoughtlessness of the English bourgeoisie and its Press with regard to pauperism, England's national epidemic.

Let us grant then that the reproaches which our "Prussian" levels at German society are well founded. Is the explanation to be sought in the unpolitical condition of Germany?

But if the bourgeoisie of unpolitical Germany cannot grasp the general significance of a partial distress, the bourgeoisie of political England, on the other hand, has managed to miss the general significance of a universal distress, which has been forced upon its attention partly by periodical recurrence in time, partly by extension in space, and partly by the failure of all efforts to remedy it.

"Prussian" further lays it to the account of the unpolitical condition of Germany that the King of Prussia finds the cause of pauperism in administrative defects or lack of benevolence, and consequently seeks the remedy for pauperism in administrative and ameliorative measures.

Is this point of view peculiar to the King of Prussia? Let us take a rapid glance at England, the only country where important political measures have been taken against pauperism.

The present English Poor Law dates from the Forty-third Act of the Government of Elizabeth. In what consisted the expedients of this legislation? In the obligation laid on parishes to support their poor workers, in the poor rate, in legal benevolence. For two hundred years this legislation—benevolence by Act of Parliament—has lasted. What is the attitude of Parliament in its Amendment Bill of 1834; after long and painful experience?

First of all, the formidable increase in pauperism is explained from a "defect in administration."

The administration of the poor rate, which consisted of officials of the respective parishes, is therefore reformed. Unions of about twenty parishes are formed, united in a single administration. A Board of Guardians, elected by taxpayers, assembles on an appointed day in the residence of the Union and decides upon the granting of relief. These boards are coordinated and supervised by officials of the Government, the Central Commission of Somerset House, the Ministry of Pauperism, Frenchman has aptly described it. The capital which this administration supervises is almost equal to the amount which the French War Office costs. The number of local administrations which it employs amounts to 500, and each of these local administrations keeps at least twelve officials busy.

The English Parliament did not stop short at the mere reform of the administration.

The chief source of the acute state of English pauperism it found in the poor law itself. Benevolence, which is the legal remedy for social crime, favours social crime. As regards pauperism in general, it is an eternal natural law, according to the theory of Malthus: "As the population unceasingly tends to overstep the means of subsistence, benevolence is folly, a public encouragement to poverty. The State can therefore do nothing more than leave poverty to its fate and at the most soften death for the poor." With this amiable theory the English Parliament combines the opinion that pauperism is poverty for which the worker is himself responsible. It should therefore not be regarded as a misfortune, but rather be suppressed and punished as a crime.

Thus the workhouse system arose, that is, the houses of the poor, whose internal arrangements deter the poverty-stricken from seeking a refuge from starvation. In the workhouse benevolence is ingeniously combined with the revenge of the bourgeoisie upon the poor who appeal to its charity.

England, therefore, at first attempted to destroy pauperism by benevolence and administrative measures. Then it perceived in the progressive increase of pauperism, not the necessary consequence of modern industry, but rather the consequence of the English poor rate. It regarded the universal distress as nothing more than a peculiarity of English legislation. What was formerly ascribed to the lack of charity was now attributed to a superfluity of charity. Finally, poverty was regarded as the fault of the poor, and punished as such.

The general significance to which pauperism has attained in political England is limited to the fact that, in course of development, in spite of the administrative measures, pauperism has grown into a national institution, and has therefore inevitably become the subject of a ramified and extensive administration, an administration, however, which no longer aims at extinguishing it, but at disciplining and perpetuating it. This administration has abandoned all thought of stopping up the source of pauperism by constructive measures; it is content to dig a grave for it with official gentleness whenever it breaks out on the surface of the official country. Instead of going beyond the administrative and charitable measures, the English State has actually gone back upon them. Its administration is confined to that pauperism which is so despairing as to allow itself to be caught and detained.

So far, therefore, "Prussian" has not demonstrated anything peculiar in the procedure of the King of Prussia. But why, exclaims the great man with rare simplicity: "Why does not the King of Prussia immediately order the education of all destitute children?" Why does he first look to the authorities and wait upon their plans and proposals?

The over-wise "Prussian" may calm himself on learning that in this respect the King of Prussia displays as little originality as in his other actions, that he has even adopted the only course that a Chief of State can adopt.

Napoleon desired to destroy mendicancy at one blow. He instructed his authorities to draw up proposals for the extirpation of mendicancy in the whole of France. The project kept him waiting; and Napoleon lost patience. Writing to his Home Secretary, Cretet, he ordered him to destroy mendicancy within one month, and said: "One should not tarry in this world without leaving behind that which would commend our memory to posterity. Do not keep me waiting another three or four months for information; you have your lawyers, your prefects, your properly trained engineers of roads and bridges, set all these to work, do not go to sleep in the usual official manner." Within a few months everything was done. On the 5th July 1808 a law was passed which put down mendicancy. How? By means of the depots, which were rapidly transformed into penal institutions, and it was not long before the poor would only reach the harbour of these institutions by way of legal punishment. And yet M. Noailles du Gard, member of the Legislative Assembly, exclaimed at the time: "Everlasting gratitude to the hero who assures a place of refuge for the needy and sustenance to the poor: childhood will no longer be neglected, poor families will no longer be deprived of their resources, nor the workers of encouragement and employment. Our steps will no longer be dogged by the disgusting spectacle of infirmities and of shameful poverty." The last cynical passage is the single truth in this eulogy.

If Napoleon asks for the views of his lawyers, prefects, and engineers, why should not the King of Prussia address himself to *his* authorities?

Why did not Napoleon order the immediate extinction of mendicancy? Of equal value is "Prussian's" question: "Why does not the King of Prussia order the immediate education of neglected children?" Does "Prussian" know what the King should have ordered? Nothing less than the immediate extinction of the proletariat. Children cannot be educated unless they are fed and freed from industrial labour. The feeding and educating of neglected children is tantamount to feeding and educating the whole adolescent proletariat, and would mean the extinction of the proletariat and of pauperism.

The Convention once had the courage to order the abolition of pauperism, yet not "immediately," as "Prussian" requires of his king, but only after it had entrusted the Committee of Public Safety with the preparation of the necessary plans and proposals, and after the latter had utilized the exhaustive investigations of the Constituent Assembly into the state of French poverty and proposed through Barrère the establishment of the *Livre de la bienfaisance nationale,* etc. What was the result of the instructions of the Convention? That there was one more order in the world and a year later starving women besieged the Convention.

The Convention, however, represented the maximum of political energy, of political power, and of political insight.

No government in the world has ever issued peremptory orders concerning pauperism, without an understanding with the authorities. The English parliament even sent commissioners into all the countries of Europe, in order to become acquainted with the various administrative remedies for pauperism. But so far as States have been concerned with pauperism, they have either confined themselves to administrative and charitable measures, or have gone back upon such measures.

Can the State behave otherwise?

The State will never find the cause of social crime in the "State and the institution of society," as "Prussian" requires of his king. Where there are political parties, each finds the cause of every evil in the fact that its opponent, instead of itself, is at the helm of the State. Even the radical and revolutionary politicians seek the cause of the evil not in the essence of the State, but in a specific form of the State, which they aim at replacing by another State form.

From the political standpoint, the State and the institution of society are not two separate things. The State is the institution of society. So far as the State recognizes social evils, it attributes them either to natural laws, which are amenable to no human power, or to the defects of private life, which is independent of the State, or in the futility of the administration which is dependent on it. Thus England finds poverty to be grounded in the natural law according to which the population is always bound to overstep the means of subsistence. According to another side, it explains pauperism from the wicked dispositions of the poor, just as the King of Prussia explained it from the unchristian sentiment of the rich, and just as the Convention explained it from the counter-revolutionary and suspicious dispositions of the property owners. England therefore punishes the poor, the King of Prussia exhorts the rich, and the Convention decapitates the property owners.

Finally, all States seek the cause of social evil in accidental or deliberate defects of administration, and therefore look to administrative measures for the remedy. Why? Just because the administration is the organized activity of the State.

The State cannot abolish the contradiction between the intentions and the good will of the administration, on the one hand, and its expedients and its resources, on the other hand, without abolishing itself, for it is based upon this contradiction. It is based upon the contradiction between public and private life, upon the contradiction between the general interest and individual interests. The administration is therefore obliged to confine itself to a formal and negative activity, for its power ceases where middle-class life and its work begin. Yes, as against the consequences which spring from the unsocial nature of this middle-class life, this private property, this trade, this industry, this mutual plundering of various middle-class circles, as against these consequences impotence is the natural law of the administration.

For this dismemberment, this slavery of middle-class society, is the natural foundation upon which the modern State rests, just as the civil society of slavery was the natural foundation upon which the antique State rested. The existence of the State is inseparable from the existence of slavery. The antique State and antique slavery—manifest classical antagonisms—were not more intimately connected than is the modern State with the modern huckstering world—sanctimonious Christian antagonisms. If the modern State wishes to abolish the impotence of its administration, it would have to abolish the present-day mode of living. If it wishes to abolish this mode of living, it would have to abolish itself, for it exists only in opposition to the same. No living person, however, would believe that defects in his existence are due to the vital principle of his life, but would rather attribute them to circumstances outside his life. Suicide is unnatural.

The State cannot therefore believe in the innate impotence of its administration. It can only take notice of formal and accidental defects therein and attempt to remedy them. If these modifications are fruitless, social crime must be a natural imperfection independent of mankind, a law of God, or else the dispositions of private individuals are too vitiated to second the good intentions of the administration. And what perverted private individuals! They murmur against the government whenever the latter restricts freedom, and they demand that the government should provide against the necessary consequences of this freedom.

The more powerful the State, and the more political, therefore, a country is, all the less is it inclined to seek in the principle of the State, and consequently in the existing institution of society, whose self-conscious and official expression the State is, for the cause of social crime, and to grasp its general principle.

Political understanding is political understanding precisely because it thinks within the limitations of politics. The more acute, the more alert it is, the more incapable it is of perceiving social crime. The classic period of political understanding is the French Revolution. Far from perceiving the source of social defects in the principle of the State, the heroes of the French Revolution rather perceived in social defects the source of political abuses. Thus Robespierre saw in great poverty and great riches only an obstacle to pure democracy. Consequently, he desired to establish a general Spartan frugality.

The principle of politics is will-power. The more one-sided, which means the more complete, political understanding is, all the more does it believe in the omnipotence of will-power, all the more blind is it to the natural and intellectual limitations to will-power, all the more incapable is it, therefore, of discovering the source of social crime.

No further proof is needed to refute the absurd hope entertained by "Prussian", according to which "political understanding" is called upon "to discover the roots of social distress in Germany."

It was ridiculous to impute to the King of Prussia a power which the Convention and Napoleon together did not possess; it was ridiculous to credit him with an insight that went beyond the limits of all politics, an insight which the wise "Prussian" possesses no more than his king.

Let us suppose that "Prussian's" observations upon the German Government and the German bourgeoisie—the latter is of course included in "German society"—are perfectly justified. Is this section of society more perplexed in Germany than in England and France? Is it possible to be more perplexed than, for example, in England, where perplexity has been elevated into a system?

If Labour revolts are now breaking out all over England, the bourgeoisie and the Government there are no better advised than in the last third of the eighteenth century. Their sole expedient is material force, and as material force diminishes in the same degree as the spread of pauperism and the insight of the proletariat increase, English perplexity necessarily grows in geometrical proportion.

Lastly, it is in point of fact untrue that the German bourgeoisie has entirely missed the general significance of the Silesian revolt.

In several towns the masters are endeavouring to combine with the journeymen. All the liberal German newspapers, the organs of the liberal bourgeoisie, are gushing about the organization of labour, the reform of society, the criticism of monopoly and of competition, etc. All this as a result of the labour movements. The newspapers of Treves, Aachen, Cologne, Wesel, Mannheim, Breslau, even of Berlin, are constantly publishing quite intelligent articles on social affairs, from which "Prussian" may learn at any time. Yes, letters from Germany are constantly expressing astonishment at the slight opposition which the bourgeoisie offers to social tendencies.

If "Prussian" had been better acquainted with the history of the social movement, he would have put his question the other way round. Why does the German bourgeoisie itself interpret the partial distress as relatively universal? Whence the animosity and cynicism of the political bourgeoisie? Whence the supineness and the sympathies of the unpolitical bourgeoisie with respect to the proletariat?

Now to "Prussian's" oracular pronouncements concerning the German workers. "The German poor," he puns, "are not wiser than the poor Germans, that is, they can nowhere see beyond their hearth, their factory, their district: the whole question has so far been neglected by the all-comprehending political soul."

In order to be able to compare the condition of the German workers with the condition of the French and English workers, "Prussian" must compare the first manifestation, the beginning of the English and French Labour movement, with the German movement which has just begun. He neglects to do this. His reasoning therefore runs upon a triviality, such as that industry in Germany is not yet so developed as in England, or that a movement in its beginnings looks different from a movement that has made progress.

If, however, "Prussian" would place himself at the correct standpoint, he would find that not any of the French and English Labour revolts possessed such a theoretical and conscious character as the Silesian weavers' revolt.

In the first place, let us recall the song of the weavers, those bold accents of the struggle, wherein hearth, factory, and district are not once mentioned, but the proletariat immediately gets into the stride of its opposition to the society of private property in the most vigorous, ruthless, and powerful fashion. The Silesian revolt begins just where the French and English Labour revolts end, with the consciousness of the being of the proletariat. The action itself bears this superior character. Not only the machines, these rivals of the worker, were destroyed, but also the ledgers, the title of property, and while all other movements have been directed in the first place against the visible enemy, the lords of industry, this movement was simultaneously directed against the bankers, the concealed foe.

Lastly, no single English Labour revolt has been conducted with equal bravery, circumspection, and persistence.

As regards the state of education or the capacity for education of the German workers generally, I may recall Weitling's excellent writings, which frequently represent an advance upon Proudhon in a theoretical respect, although they may be inferior to him in finish. Where can the bourgeoisie—their philosophers and scholars included—show a work similar to Weitling's "Guarantees of Harmony and Freedom" pertaining to the emancipation of the bourgeoisie—the political emancipation? If we compare the mediocrity of German political literature with this expansive and brilliant literary début of the German worker; if we compare this giant child's shoe of the proletariat with the dwarf proportions of the worn-out political shoe of the German bourgeoisie, we must predict an athletic figure for the German Cinderella. It must be admitted that the German proletariat is the theorist of the European proletariat, just as the English proletariat is its political economist, and the French proletariat its politician. Germany possesses a classical vocation for the social revolution although she is incapable of the political revolution. For if the impotence of the German bourgeoisie is the same thing as the political impotence of Germany, the talent of the German proletariat—even apart from German theory—is the social talent of Germany. The disproportion between the philosophical and the political development in Germany is no abnormality. It is a necessary disproportion. Only by means of socialism can a philosophical people put its philosophy into practice, and only in the proletariat, therefore, can it find the active element for its emancipation.

At this moment, however, I have neither the time nor the inclination to explain to "Prussian" the relation of "German society" to the social transformation, and from this relation to explain, on the one side, the weak reaction of the German bourgeoisie to socialism, and, on the other hand, the exceptional talent of the German proletariat for socialism. The first elements for the understanding of this phenomenon he will find in my introduction to the criticism of Hegel's philosophy of right ("Franco-German Annuals"). (See pp. 11 *et seq.* of this book.)

The wisdom of the German poor is therefore in inverse proportion to the wisdom of the poor Germans. Thus "Prussian's" attempt to manipulate his thought in the form of antithesis on the occasion of the Silesian labour unrest had led to the greatest antithesis against the truth. What a thoughtful mind should do in connection with a first outbreak, such as the Silesian workers' revolt, is not to play the schoolmaster to this event, but to study its peculiar character. For this a certain amount of scientific insight and some goodwill is necessary, whereas for the other operation a glib phraseology, saturated in shallow egoism, fully suffices.

Why does "Prussian" judge the German workers so contemptuously? Because he finds that the "whole question,"—namely the question of labour distress—has not yet been taken up by the "all-comprehending political soul." He carries his Platonic love to the political soul so far as to say:

"All revolts which break out from the isolation of men from the community and the separation of their thoughts from the social principles will be extinguished in blood and unreason; but if the distress first creates the understanding, and if the political understanding of the Germans discovers the roots of social distress, then these incidents would also be felt in Germany as the symptom of a great transformation."

In the first half of the sentence we read: if distress creates understanding, and in the second half: if political understanding discovers the roots of social distress. Simple understanding in the first half of the antithesis becomes political understanding in the second half, just as the simple distress of the first half of the antithesis becomes social distress in the second half. Why has the artist in style so unequally endowed the two halves of the antithesis?

Had "Prussian" written: "If social distress creates political understanding, and if political understanding discovers the roots of social distress," the absurdity of this antithesis could not have escaped any impartial reader. Such a reader would have immediately wondered why the anonymous writer did not couple social understanding with social distress and political understanding with political distress, as the simplest logic dictates? Now to business.

So false is it to say that social distress creates political understanding that the truth is rather the reverse; social well-being creates political understanding. Political understanding is an intellectual quality and is given to him who already has, who lives in clover. Our "Prussian" should hear what a French political economist, M. Michel Chevalier, has to say upon this subject: "In the year 1789 when the bourgeoisie revolted, the sole thing they wanted was a share in the government of the country. Emancipation consisted in snatching the direction of public affairs, the high civic, military and religious functions,

75

from the hands of the privileged persons who possessed the monopoly of these functions. Wealthy and enlightened, able to govern themselves, they desired to escape from the *régime du bon plaisir*."

How incapable political understanding is of discovering the source of social distress we have already demonstrated to "Prussian." Another word about this opinion of his. The more cultivated and general the political understanding of a people is, all the more does the proletariat—at least at the beginning of the movement—dissipate its energies in irrational, useless, and brutally suppressed revolts. Because it thinks along political lines, it perceives the cause of all evils in the wills of men, and all remedies to lie in force and the overthrow of a particular form of the State. In proof whereof we cite the first outbreak of the French proletariat. The workers in Lyons believed they were only pursuing political aims and were only soldiers of the Republic, whereas they were in truth soldiers of socialism. Thus their political understanding hid from them the roots of social distress; it distorted their insight into their real aims; their political understanding deceived their social instinct.

"Prussian" prophesies the suppression of revolts which break out owing to the "isolation of men from the community and the separation of their thoughts from social principles."

We have shown that the Silesian revolt was by no means characterized by the separation of ideas from social principles. It remains to deal with the "isolation of men from the community." By community is to be understood in this connection the political community, the State institution. It is the old story of unpolitical Germany.

But do not all revolts without exception break out from the isolation of men from the community? Does not every revolt necessarily presuppose this isolation? Would the Revolution of 1789 have taken place without the isolation of the French citizens from the community? Its aim, in fact, was to end this isolation.

But the community from which the worker is isolated is a community of quite a different nature from and of quite other dimensions than the political community. This community, from which his own labour separates him, is life itself, physical and intellectual life, human morality, human activity, human enjoyment, the human community.

Human life is the real community of men. Just as the isolation from this body is more complete, more painful, more to be feared, more contradictory than is isolation from the political community, so too the removal of this isolation, and even a partial reaction, a revolt against the same, are tasks all the more infinite as man is more infinite than the citizen, and human life than political life. However partial the industrial revolt may be, it conceals within itself a universal soul: political revolt may be never so universal but it hides a narrow-minded spirit under the most colossal form.

"Prussian" worthily closes his article with the following phrase: "A social revolution without a political soul (that is, without organized insight from the standpoint of the whole) is impossible."

We have seen that a social revolution maybe considered to be from the standpoint of the whole because, even if it only occurs in a factory district, it is a protest of men against degraded life, because it proceeds from the standpoint of the real individual, because the community against whose separation from himself the individual reacts, is the real community of men, the civic community.

The political soul of a revolution, on the other hand, consists in the endeavour of the classes without political influence to abolish their isolation from the community and from government. Their standpoint is that of the State, an abstract whole, which exists only in and through its separation from real life, which is unthinkable without the organized antagonism between the general idea and the individual existence of man. Consequently a revolution of political souls organizes a ruling clique in society, in accordance with the limited and doubly-cleft nature of these souls, at the cost of society.

We should like to confide to "Prussian" what a "social revolution with a political soul" is; we should like at the same time to suggest to him that not once has he been able to raise himself above the restricted political standpoint.

A "social" revolution with a political soul is either a composite absurdity, if "Prussian" means by "social" revolution a social revolution in contrast to a political, and yet invests the social revolution with a political, instead of a social, soul. Or a "social revolution with a political soul" is nothing but what is otherwise called a "political revolution" or a "revolution pure and simple."

Every revolution dissolves the old society; in so far it is social. Every revolution overthrows the old power; in so far it is political.

"Prussian" may choose between the paraphrase and the absurdity.

Equally ridiculous is the notion of a political revolution with a social soul. The revolution as such—the overthrow of the existing power and the dissolution of the old conditions—is a political act. But without a revolution, socialism cannot be enforced. It requires this political act, so far as it has need of the process of destruction and dissolution. But where its organizing activity begins, where its proper aim, its soul, emerges, there socialism casts away the political hull.

MORALIZING CRITICISM AND CRITICAL MORALITY: A POLEMIC AGAINST KARL HEINZEN

"I cannot imagine that Mr Engels and our communists are so blind as not to see that force also dominates property, and that the injustice in the property relations is only maintained by force. I call that person a fool and a coward who cherishes animosity towards a bourgeois because he is accumulating money, and leaves a king in peace because he has acquired power," states Mr Heinzen.

"Force also dominates property." Property is likewise also a species of power. The economists call capital, for example, "the command over other labour." We are thus confronted with two kinds of force or power: on the one hand, the power of property, that is, of the property owner; on the other hand, the political power, the State power. "Force also dominates property" means that property has not yet got the political power in its hands, but is rather vexed by it, for example, by arbitrary taxes, by confiscation, by privileges, by the disturbing interference of the bureaucracy in industry and trade and the like.

In other words: The bourgeoisie is not yet politically constituted as a class. The State power is not yet its own power. In countries where the bourgeoisie has already conquered political power, and where political rule is nothing less than the rule, not of the individual bourgeois over the workers, but of the bourgeois class over the whole of society, Mr Heinzen's dictum has lost its meaning. The propertyless are, of course, not affected by political rule, so far as it relates directly to property.

Whilst, therefore, Mr Heinzen fancies he is uttering a truth as eternal as it is original, he has only recorded the fact that the German bourgeoisie must capture the political power, that is, he is saying unconsciously what Engels says, in the brave belief that he is saying the opposite.

"The injustice in the property relations," continues Mr Heinzen, "is only maintained by force." Either Mr Heinzen understands by "the injustice in the property relations" the above-mentioned pressure, which the German bourgeoisie still suffers in its "most sacred" interests from the absolute monarchy, and then he only repeats what has just been said—or he understands by "the injustice in the property relations" the economic relations of the workers, and in that case his revelation amounts to this: The existing bourgeois property relations are "maintained" by the State power, which the bourgeoisie has organized for the protection of its property relations. The proletarians must, therefore, overthrow the political power where it is already in the hands of the bourgeoisie. They must themselves attain to power, to revolutionary power. Mr Heinzen again says unconsciously what Engels says, again in the sincere conviction of having said the opposite. What he says he does not mean, and what he means he does not say.

Moreover, if the bourgeoisie politically, that is, through the agency of its State power, maintains "the injustice in the property relations," it does not create the latter. The "injustice in the property relations," conditioned by the modern division of labour, the modern form of exchange, competition, concentration, etc., does not in any way proceed from the political rule of the bourgeoisie, but, contrariwise, the political rule of the bourgeoisie proceeds from these modern relations of production, which are proclaimed by the bourgeois economists to be necessary and eternal laws.

If, therefore, the proletariat should overthrow the political rule of the bourgeoisie, its victory would be only temporary, only an episode in the service of the bourgeois revolution, so long as the material conditions which would render necessary the abolition of the bourgeois mode of production, and consequently the definitive overthrow of the political rule of the bourgeoisie, had not yet been created in the course of historical development. From this point of view, the Reign of Terror in France did no more than to clear away the feudal ruins from French soil by its hammer blows.

The anxious and cautious bourgeoisie would have taken decades to perform this work. The bloody action of the people, therefore, prepared the way. Similarly, the overthrow of the absolute monarchy would have been merely a momentary incident, if the economic conditions for the rule of the bourgeois class had not been developed to the point of ripeness.

Men built for themselves a new world, not out of earthly goods, as the bluff Heinzen superstition would have us believe, but out of the historical achievements of their shipwrecked world. In the course of development, they have first to create the material conditions for a new society themselves, and no effort of the mind or the will can save them from this destiny.

It is typical of bluff common sense that where it manages to see difference, it does not see unity, and where it sees unity, it does not see difference. If perchance it sets up distinguishing qualities, it immediately petrifies them, and sees nothing but sophistry in the notion of rubbing these slabs of ideas against each other until they catch fire.

In stating that money and force, property and rule, money-making and power-acquiring are not the same, it is merely uttering a tautology.

How "money-making" is turned into "winning power," and "property" into "political rule," and how, instead of the hard and fast distinctions drawn by Mr Heinzen, the two forces are interrelated to the point of unity, of all this he may quickly convince himself by observing how the communes purchased their municipal rights; how the citizens enticed money out of the pockets of the feudal lords by trade and industry, on the one hand, and disintegrated their landed property by bills of exchange, on the other hand; aiding absolute monarchy to triumph over the great feudatories who were thus being undermined, just as later they exploited the financial crises of absolute monarchy itself, etc.; how the most absolute monarch became dependent on the Stock Exchange barons through the national debt system—a product of modern industry and of modern commerce; and how in the international relations of peoples industrial monopoly is immediately transmuted into political rule, as in the case of the princes of the Holy Alliance in the "German liberation war," who were only the paid foot soldiers of England, etc., etc.

Mr Heinzen cannot fail to notice that even in Prussia the power of property has been raised to the point of a *mariage forcé* with the political power. Listen further:

"You wish to give a contemporary meaning to social questions; and yet you fail to see that there is no more important question than that of monarchy versus republic." A little while ago Mr Heinzen only saw the *distinction* between the money power and the political power, now he only sees *unity* between political questions and social questions.

The political relations of men are, of course, also social relations, as are all relations which bind men to men. All questions pertaining to the relations of men to each other are social questions at the same time.

The "social questions" which have been "discussed in our time" increase in importance in the degree that we emerge from the realm of absolute monarchy. Socialism and communism did not originate in Germany, but in England, France and North America. The first appearance of a really active communist party may be placed within the period of the middle-class revolution, the moment when constitutional monarchy was abolished. The most consistent republicans, in England the Levellers, in France Babeuf, Buonarotti, etc., were the first to proclaim these "social questions." The "Conspiracy of Babeuf," written by his friend and comrade Buonarotti, shows how these republicans derived their social insight from the "historical movement." It also demonstrates that when the social question of princedom versus republic is removed, not a single social question of the kind that interests the proletariat has been solved.

The property question as it presents itself in "our time" cannot be recognized under the form in which Mr Heinzen clothes it, *i.e.* "whether it is right that one man should possess everything and another nothing, whether man as an individual need possess anything at all," and suchlike simple questions of conscience and pious phrases.

The question of property assumes different forms according to the successive stages of development of industry in general and according to its particular stages of development in various countries.

For the Galician peasant, for example, the property question reduces itself to the transformation of feudal landed property into small middle-class holdings. It has for him the same meaning as it had for the French peasants of 1789. On the other hand, the English agricultural labourer does not stand in any relation to the landed proprietor. He comes into contact merely with the farmer, that is, the industrial capitalist who carries on agriculture upon factory lines. This industrial capitalist, on his part, who pays a rent to the land owner, stands in a direct relationship to the latter. The abolition of landed property is therefore the most important property question that exists for the English industrial bourgeoisie, and the struggle against the Corn Laws had no other meaning. The abolition of capital, on the other hand, is the property question as understood equally by the English agricultural labourer and by the English factory worker.

Both in the English and in the French Revolutions the property question presented itself in such wise that it seemed to be imperative to enforce free competition and to effect the abolition of all feudal property relations, such as manorial rights, guilds, monopolies, which had been transformed into fetters upon the industry which was developing between the sixteenth and eighteenth centuries. Lastly, in "our time" the property question means the abolition of the antagonisms which are produced by the great industry, the development of the world market and of free competition.

The property question, according to the successive stages in the development of industry, has always been the life question of a particular class. In the seventeenth and eighteenth centuries when the point at issue was the abolition of feudal property relations, the property question was the life question of the bourgeois class. In the nineteenth century, when the point at issue is the abolition of bourgeois property relations, the property question is a life question for the working class.

The property question, which in "our time" is a world-historical question, has therefore a meaning only in the modern bourgeois society. The more developed this society is, the more therefore the bourgeoisie develops itself economically in a country, and consequently the more the State power has assumed a bourgeois expression, all the more acutely does the social question obtrude itself, in France more acutely than in Germany, in England more acutely than in France, in the constitutional monarchy more acutely than in the absolute monarchy, in the Republic more acutely than in the constitutional monarchy. Thus, for example, the crises in the credit system and in speculation, etc., are nowhere more acute than in North America. Nowhere, too, does social inequality obtrude itself more harshly than in the Eastern States of North America, because it is nowhere less glossed over by political inequality. If pauperism has not yet developed here to the extent that it has in England, this is due to economic conditions which need not be further discussed at this place. Meanwhile pauperism is making the most delightful progress.

"In a country where there is no privileged class, where all classes of society have equal rights" (but the difficulty lies in the existence of classes), "and where our population is far from pressing on the means of subsistence, it is in fact alarming to see pauperism growing with such rapidity." (Report of Mr

Meredith to the Pennsylvanian Congress.) "It is proved that pauperism in Massachusetts has increased by 60 per cent, in twenty-five years." (From Miles' Register.)

As in England under the name of Chartists, so in North America under the name of National Reformers, the workers are forming a political party, whose slogan is not—monarchy versus republic, but rule of the working class versus rule of the bourgeois class.

While therefore it is just in the modern bourgeois society, with its corresponding political forms of the constitutional or the republican representative state, that the "property question" has become the most important "social question," it is the peculiar situation of the German middle-class man which prompts him to assert that the question of princedom is the most important social question of the time.

"The princes," Mr Heinzen tells us, are the "chief authors of all poverty and all distress." Where princedom has been abolished, this explanation is of course out of place, and the slavery system upon which the ancient republics broke down—the slavery system which will lead to the most terrible collisions in the southern states of republican North America, the slavery system may exclaim with Jack Falstaff: and if reasons were as plentiful as blackberries!

Once upon a time the people were obliged to place at their head the most eminent personalities to conduct public affairs. Later these positions were transmitted through families. And lastly the stupidity and depravity of mankind have tolerated this abuse for centuries. If a conference were convened of all the native pot-house politicians of Europe, they could answer nothing different. And if one went through Mr Heinzen's entire works, they would yield no other answer.

Bluff commonsense believes that it explains princedom by declaring itself to be the latter's opponent. But the difficulty which confronts this normal method of reasoning is to show how the opponent of healthy commonsense and of moral dignity came to be born, and to drag out a remarkably tenacious life for centuries. Nothing simpler. For centuries healthy commonsense and moral dignity were non-existent. In other words, the sense and the morality of centuries answered to the institution of princedom, instead of contradicting it. And even this sense and this morality of bygone centuries are not understood by the "healthy commonsense" of to-day. The latter does not grasp it, and therefore despises it. It flees from history to morality, which allows it full play to the heavy artillery of its moral indignation.

In the same fashion as political "healthy commonsense" here explains the rise and continuance of princedom as the work of unreason, in the same way religious "healthy commonsense" explains heresy and unbelief as the work of the devil. In the same manner irreligious "healthy commonsense" explains religion as the work of the devil, of the parsons.

But once Mr Heinzen has explained the origin of princedom by means of moral commonplaces, the "connection of princedom with social conditions" follows quite naturally. Listen: "An individual sequestrates the state, and more or less sacrifices a whole people, not only materially, but also morally, to his person and his supporters, institutes a graduated series of ranks, divides the people, as if they were fat and lean cattle, into various classes, and, solely on the ground of affection for his own person, makes every member of the State the official enemy of the other."

Mr Heinzen has in mind the princes upon the top of the social structure in Germany. He does not doubt for a moment that they have made and are daily renewing their social foundation. Can a simpler explanation be afforded of the connection of the monarchy with social conditions, of which it is the official political expression, than by making this connection the work of the princes? What is the connection between representative chambers and the modern middle-class society which they represent? The former have made the latter. Similarly political divine right with its apparatus and its gradations has made the profane world, of which it is the holy of holies. By a parity of reasoning religious divine right has made the secular conditions of which it constitutes a fantastic and glorified reflexion.

Bluff commonsense, which proffers such homely wisdom with beseeming pathos would of course be morally indignant at the opponent who attempted to show that the apple did not make the apple tree.

Modern historical research has shown how absolute monarchy appeared in the period of transition, when the old feudal classes were decaying and the medieval burgher class was evolving into the modern bourgeois class, without either of the disputing parties being able to settle accounts with the other.

The elements out of which absolute monarchy builds itself up cannot in any way be its product: they rather form its preliminary condition, the historic origin of which is too well known to be repeated here. That absolute monarchy in Germany developed later and is lasting longer is to be explained by reference to the distorted course of development of the German middle class. The solution to the riddle of this course of development is to be found in the history of commerce and industry.

The decay of the German free towns, the destruction of the Order of Knighthood, the defeat of the peasants—the local supremacy of the princes which arose therefrom—the decay of German industry and of German commerce, which were based on entirely medieval conditions, at the same time as the modern world market was being opened up and large-scale manufacture was thriving—the depopulation and the barbarous condition that followed in the wake of the Thirty Years War—the character of the reviving national branches of industry, such as the small linen industry, which are adapted to patriarchal conditions and relations—the nature of the articles of export, the greater part of which belonged to agriculture, and therefore almost alone increased the material sources of life of the landed nobility, and consequently the power of the latter over the citizens—the depressed position of Germany in the world market in general, whereby the subsidies paid by foreigners to the princes became a chief source of national income, the consequent dependence of the citizens upon the Court, etc. etc.,—all these conditions, within which German society and a political organization corresponding thereto developed, are transformed by Heinzen's bluff common sense into a few pithy sayings, the pith of which consists in the assertion that "German princedom" made and daily remakes "German society."

The optimistic delusion which enables healthy common sense to find in princedom the source of German society, instead of seeing the source of princedom in German society, is susceptible of an easy explanation.

It sees truly enough at first glance, and its first glance is always keenest, that the German princes maintain and consolidate the old German social condition, upon which their existence stands or falls, and forcibly react against the dissolving elements. It likewise sees, on the other hand, the dissolving elements striving with the princely power. All the healthy five senses testify at once that princedom is the foundation of the old society, its gradations, its prejudices, and its antagonisms.

Regarded more closely, however, this phenomenon only contradicts the rough and ready opinion for which it furnished the innocent occasion.

The powerful reactionary role which princedom assumed only proves that in the pores of the old society a new society has evolved, which feels the political husk—the appropriate covering of the old society—to be an unnatural fetter which it must burst. The more immature these new elements are, the more conservative appears to be even the most vigorous reaction of the old political power. The reaction of princedom, instead of proving that it makes the old society, rather proves that it is at the end of its tether so soon as the material conditions of the old society are obsolete. Its reaction is at the same time the reaction of the old society, which is still the official society.

If the material conditions of life of society have so far developed that the transformation of their official political shape has become a vital necessity for it, the entire physiognomy of the old political power undergoes a transformation. Thus absolute monarchy now aims at decentralization, instead of at centralization, wherein consists its proper civilizing activity.

Itself the product of the defeat of the feudal orders, and even taking the most active part in their destruction, it tries now to retain at least the semblance of feudal distinctions. Formerly favouring commerce and industry and also the rise of the burgher class, as being necessary conditions both of the national power and of its own brilliance, absolute monarchy now puts all kinds of obstacles in the way of commerce and industry, which have become more and more dangerous weapons in the hands of a powerful bourgeoisie. From the town, which fostered its rise, it casts an anxious and dulled glance over the countryside, which is fertilized with the corpses of its old heroic foes.

But what Mr Heinzen understands by the "connection of politics with social conditions" is really only the connection of German princedom with German distress and German poverty.

The monarchy, like every other State, exists externally for the working class only in the form of taxes. Taxes constitute the existence of the State economically expressed. Officials and parsons, soldiers and ballet dancers, schoolmasters and beadles, Greek museums and Gothic towers, civil list and army list—the communal seeds wherein all these fabulous existences embryonically slumber are—the taxes.

And what reasoning citizen would not refer the starving people to the taxes, to the ill-gotten gains of the princes, as the source of their poverty? German princes and German distress! In other words, the taxes on which the princes live in opulence and which the people pay with the sweat of their blood! What inexhaustible material for declamatory human saviours!

No doubt the monarchy is very expensive. One has only to glance at the North American budget and compare it with what our thirty-eight duodecimo fatherland has to pay in order to be administered and over-disciplined.

The blustering outbreaks of this conceited demagogy are answered not by the communists, but by such middle-class economists as Ricardo, Senior, etc., in a few words.

The economic existence of the State is the taxes. The economic existence of the worker is wages. What has to be settled is the relation between wages and taxes.

The average wage is necessarily reduced by competition to the minimum, that is, to a wage which allows the workers and their race to drag out a scanty existence. Taxes form a part of this minimum, for the political business of the worker just consists in paying taxes. If the whole of the taxes that fall on the working class were drastically cut down, the necessary consequence would be that wages would be reduced by the whole amount of the taxes now included in them. Either the profit of the employer would thereby be increased to the same extent, or a change in the method of raising taxes would have taken place. Instead of the capitalist advancing to-day in wages the taxes which the worker must pay, he would no longer pay them in this roundabout fashion, but directly to the State. If wages are higher in North America than in Europe, this is by no means due to its lighter taxation. It is the consequence of its territorial, commercial, and industrial situation. The demand for workers in relation to the supply of workers is considerably greater than in Europe. And this truth is known already to every pupil of Adam Smith.

On the other hand, so far as the bourgeoisie is concerned, both the incidence and the nature of the taxes, as well as the spending of the money, are a vital question, both on account of their influence upon commerce and industry, and because taxes are the golden cord with which absolute monarchy is strangled.

After vouchsafing such profound explanations about the "connection of politics with social conditions" and the "class relations" with the State power, Mr Heinzen exclaims triumphantly: "The 'communistic narrow-mindedness' which divides men into classes, or antagonizes them according to their handicraft, has been avoided by me. I have left open the 'possibility' that 'humanity' is not always determined by 'class' or the 'length of one's purse.'" Bluff common sense transforms the class distinction into the "length of the purse" and the class antagonism into trade quarrels. The length of the purse is a purely quantitative distinction, which may perchance antagonize any two individuals of the same class. That the medieval guilds confronted each other on the basis of handicraft is well known. But it is likewise well known that the modern class distinction is by no means based on handicraft; rather the division of labour within the same class produces very different methods of work.

It is very 'possible' that particular individuals are not always influenced in their attitude by the class to which they belong, but this has as little effect upon the class struggle as the secession of a few nobles to the *tiers état* had on the French Revolution. And then these nobles at least joined a class, the revolutionary class, the bourgeoisie. But Mr Heinzen sees all classes melt away before the solemn idea of 'humanity.'

If he believes that entire classes, which are based upon economic conditions independent of their will, and are set by these conditions in a relation of mutual antagonism, can break away from their real relations, by virtue of the quality of 'humanity' which is inherent in all men, how easy it should be for a prince to raise himself above his 'princedom', above his 'princely handicraft' by virtue of 'humanity'? Why does he take it amiss when Engels perceives a 'brave Emperor Joseph' behind his revolutionary phrases?

But if, on the one hand, Mr Heinzen obliterates all distinctions, in addressing himself vaguely to the 'humanity' of Germans, so that he is obliged to include even the princes in his admonitions, on the other hand, he finds himself obliged to set up at least one distinction among Germans, for without a distinction there can be no antagonism, and without an antagonism, no materials for political Capuchinian sermons.

Mr Heinzen therefore divides Germans into princes and subjects.

The 'narrow-minded' communists see not only the political distinction of prince and subject, but also the social distinction of classes.

It is well known that, shortly after the July Revolution, the victorious bourgeoisie, in its September laws, made "the incitement of class against class," probably also out of 'humanity,' a criminal offence, to which imprisonment and fines were attached. It is further well known that the English bourgeois newspapers could not denounce the Chartist leaders and Chartist writers more effectively than by reproaching them with setting class against class. It is even notorious that, in consequence of inciting class against class, German writers are incarcerated in fortresses. Is not Mr Heinzen this time talking the language of the French September laws, the English bourgeois newspapers, and the German penal code?

But no. The well-meaning Mr Heinzen only fears that the communists "are seeking to assure the princes a revolutionary Fontanelle." Thus the Belgian liberals assure us that the radicals are in secret alliance with the catholics; the French liberals assure us that the democrats have an understanding with the legitimists. And the liberal Mr Heinzen assures us that the communists have an understanding with the princes.

As I once pointed out in the Franco-German Annuals, Germany has her own Christian-Germanic plague. Her bourgeoisie was so retarded in its development that it is beginning its struggle with absolute monarchy and seeking to establish its political power at the moment when in all developed countries the bourgeoisie is already engaged in the most violent struggles with the working class, and when its political illusions are already obsolete so far as the intellect of Europe is concerned.

In this country, where the political poverty of absolute monarchy still exists with a whole appendage of decayed semi-feudal orders and conditions, there exist on the other hand, partly in consequence of the industrial development and Germany's dependence on the world market, the antagonisms between the bourgeoisie and the working class, and the struggle arising therefrom, an instance of which are the workers' revolts in Silesia and Bohemia. The German bourgeoisie therefore finds itself in a relation of antagonism to the proletariat before it has yet constituted itself politically as a class. The struggle among the subjects has broken out before ever princes and nobles have been got rid of, in spite of all Hambach songs.

Mr Heinzen does not know how to explain these contradictory relations, which of course are also reflected in German literature, except by putting them on to his opponents' conscience and interpreting them as the consequence of the counter-revolutionary activities of the communists.

Meanwhile the German workers are quite aware that the absolute monarchy does not and cannot hesitate one moment to greet them with a whiff of grapeshot in the service of the bourgeoisie. Why then should they prefer the direct rule of the bourgeoisie to the brutal oppression of absolute government, with its semi-feudal retinue? The workers know that the bourgeoisie must not only make them wider concessions than absolute monarchy, but that in the interests of its commerce and industry, the bourgeoisie must create against its will the conditions for the unity of the workers, and the unity of the workers is the first requisite for their victory. The workers know that the abolition of bourgeois property relations is not brought about by the maintenance of feudal property relations. They know their own revolutionary movement can only be accelerated through the revolutionary movement of the bourgeoisie against the feudal orders and the absolute monarchy. They know that their own struggle with the bourgeoisie can only break out on the day the bourgeoisie triumphs. In spite of all, they do not share Mr Heinzen's middle-class illusions. They can and must take part in the middle-class revolution as a condition preliminary to the Labour revolution. But they cannot for a moment regard it as their objective.

That the attitude of the workers is as above described, of this the English Chartists have furnished us with a brilliant example in the recent Anti-Corn Law League movement. Not for a moment did they believe the lies and delusions of the middle-

93

class radicals, not for a moment did they abandon their struggle against the latter, but fully conscious of what they were doing, the Chartists assisted their enemies to triumph over the Tories, and the day after the abolition of the Corn Laws, it was no longer Tories and Free Traders who faced each other at the hustings, but Free Traders and Chartists. And they captured seats in Parliament from these middle-class radicals.

Mr Heinzen understands the middle-class liberals just as little as he understands the workers, however unconsciously he labours in their service. He believes it necessary to repeat to them the old platitudes anent German "laziness" and humility. But the honest man takes quite seriously what are only servile phrases in the mouth of a Camphausen or a Hansemann. The bourgeois gentry will laugh at this simplicity. They know that the mob is bold and aggressive in revolutions. Consequently, the bourgeois gentry try as far as possible to transform the absolute monarchy into a middle-class monarchy by amicable means.

But absolute monarchy in Prussia, as formerly in England and France, does not lend itself to peaceful transformation into a middle-class monarchy. It does not gracefully abdicate. In addition to personal prejudices, the princes are bound hand and foot by a whole civil, military, and parsonic bureaucracy—constituent parts of absolute monarchy which do not by any means desire to exchange their ruling position for a serving position under the bourgeoisie.

On the other hand, the feudal orders hold aloof, as what is at stake is their existence or non-existence, that is, property or expropriation. It is clear that absolute monarchy, in spite of all the servile homage of the bourgeoisie, perceives its true interest to lie on the side of these orders.

As little, therefore, as the sweet persuasions of a Lally Tollendal, a Mounier, a Malouet, or a Mirabeau could induce a Louis XVI. to cast in his lot with the bourgeoisie, in opposition to the feudalists and the remnants of absolute monarchy, just as little will the siren songs of a Camphausen or a Hansemann convince Friedrich Wilhelm IV.

But Mr Heinzen has no concern either with the bourgeoisie or with the proletariat in Germany. His party is the "party of humanity," that is the honest and warmhearted enthusiasts who champion middle-class interests under the disguise of "human" objects, without being clear as to the connection of the idealistic phrase with its realistic content.

To his party, the party of man, or the crowd of humanity in Germany, the State builder Karl Heinzen offers the "best republic," the best republic devised by him, "the federal republic with social institutions." Rousseau once sketched the best political world for the Poles and Mably for the Corsicans. The great Genevese citizen has found a still greater successor.

"I submit that just as a flower can only be made out of petals, so a republic can only be composed of republican elements." A man who knows how to make flowers out of petals, even if it is only a daisy, cannot fail to devise the best republic, whatever an ill-natured world might say.

In spite of all slanderous tongues, the brave state builder takes the example of the Charter of Republican North America. What seems offensive to him, he brushes aside with his common sense. Thus he accomplishes a revised edition—in *usum delphini*, that is for the use and edification of "German humanity." The colossal picture of the world devised by him he has in fact hung up with his own hand on the highest summit of the Swiss Alps.

Cacatum non est pictum, hisses the voice of the "small" impenitent snake. And the republican Ajax angrily lets the communistic Thersites fall to the ground, and blurts out in a deep-throated voice the fearful words: "You carry the ridiculous too far, Mr Engels!"

And really, Mr Engels? Do you not believe that the American federal system is the best political form which statecraft has so far devised? You shake your head? What? You deny that the American federal system has ever been devised by statecraft at all? And that there are "best political social forms" *in abstracto?* But that is the last straw.

You are shameless enough to point out to us that the honest German who would benefit his true fatherland by conferring on it the North American constitution, beautified and improved, resembles the idiotic merchant who copied the ledgers of his rich rival, and imagined that being in possession of this copy, he had also come into possession of the coveted wealth.

Barbaroux, and other persons who had made much noise in the world, were made shorter by a whole head because they happened to claim the "American federal system" to be the "best political form." And thus it will befall all other Goliaths to whom it may occur, in the midst of any democratic revolution in Europe, and especially in still quite feudal and dismembered Germany, to put the "American federal system" in place of the one and indivisible republic and its levelling centralization.

The state-founding Hercules indeed does not copy slavishly the North American federal republic. He decorates it with "social institutions"; he would regulate the property relations "according to rational principles," and the seven great measures wherewith he would abolish the old bourgeois society are by no means wretched flimsy recipes collected from modern, objectionable communist and socialist cookshops.

To the "Incas" and "Campe's books for children" the great Karl Heinzen is indebted for his recipe for the "humanizing of society," just as he is indebted for the latter pompous phrase not to the philosopher and Pomeranian Ruge, but rather to a "Peruvian" grown grey in wisdom. And Mr Engels calls all this arbitrarily-contrived, commonplace enthusiasm for world improvement.

Take for instance any well-meaning citizen and ask him on his conscience: What is the difficulty under which the existing property relations labour? And the worthy man will place his index finger at the tip of his nose, draw two deep breaths of thought, and then give it out as his opinion, that it is a shame for many to possess "nothing," not even the most absolute necessities, while others roll in shameless millions, not only to the detriment of the propertyless masses, but also to that of honest citizens. *Aurea mediocritas.* Golden mediocrity, the worthy member of the middle class will exclaim. It is only extremes that should be avoided. What rational state constitution would be compatible with these extremes, these highly objectionable extremes?

And now take a look at the Heinzen "federal republic," with "social institutions" and seven measures for the "humanizing of society." There a minimum of property is assured to every citizen, below which he cannot fall, and a maximum of property is prescribed which he must not exceed. Has Mr Heinzen then not solved all difficulties inasmuch as he has repeated in the form of State decrees and thereby realized the pious desire of all worthy citizens, that none should have too little and none too much?

And in the same equally simple and generous fashion Mr Heinzen solves all the economic problems. He has regulated property according to reasonable principles corresponding to honest cheapness.

And do not raise the objection that the "rational rules" of property are just those "economic laws" on whose cold-blooded necessity all cheap "measures," whether or not recommended by Incas and Campe's books for children and held in great esteem by the most sturdy patriots, must come to grief.

How unkind it is to raise economic objections against a man who, unlike others, does not boast of his "studies of political economy," but has rather out of modesty managed to give the impression in all his works, that he has still to make his first studies in political economy.

Whereas private property is not a simple relation, or even an abstract concept, a principle, but consists in the totality of middle-class production relations—we are concerned here not with subordinate and decaying, but with existing, middle-class private property—whereas all these middle-class productive relations are class relations, a connection which is obvious to every pupil of Adam Smith or Ricardo—an alteration in these conditions can only be brought about by an alteration of these classes in their reciprocal connection, and an alteration in the position of classes is—a historical change, a product of the total social activity, the product of a specific "historical movement."

For example, in order to explain the abolition of middle-class property relations, modern historians would have to describe the movement in which the bourgeoisie progressed to the point where it had developed its conditions of life far enough to be able to abolish the whole of the feudal orders and the feudal mode of existence, and consequently the feudal relations of production within which these feudal orders had been producing. The abolition of feudal property relations and the foundation of modern middle-class society was therefore not the result of a certain action which proceeded from a particular theoretical principle pressed to its logical conclusion. The principles and theories which the writers of the bourgeoisie put forward during the latter's struggle with feudalism were rather nothing but the theoretical expression of the practical movement. How this expression was more or less Utopian, dogmatic, or doctrinaire, according as it related to a more or less developed phase of the real movement can be clearly traced.

Proudhon

Just as the first critical moves in every science are necessarily entangled in the assumptions of the science which they are intending to combat, so Proudhon's work *Qu'est ce que la propriété?* is a criticism of political economy from the standpoint of political economy. Since the criticism of political economy forms the chief subject of interest, we need not here examine the legal section of the book, which criticizes law from the standpoint of law. Proudhon's book is therefore scientifically surpassed by the critical school of political economy, even of political economy as conceived by Proudhon. This work of criticism was only rendered possible by Proudhon himself, just as Proudhon's criticism had as its antecedents the criticism of the mercantile system by the physiocrats, that of the physiocrats by Adam Smith, that of Adam Smith by Ricardo, as well as the labours of Fourier and Saint-Simon.

All the developments of political economy have private property as their major premise. This fundamental assumption is regarded by it as an unassailable fact, which needs no demonstration, and about which it only chances to speak casually, as M. Say naively confesses.

Now Proudhon subjects private property, the basis of political economy, to a critical examination, which is in fact the first decisive, ruthless, and at the same time scientific analysis. This constitutes the great scientific progress which he made, a progress which revolutionized political economy, and first rendered possible a real science of political economy.

Proudhon's work *Qu'est ce que la propriété?* has the same significance for modern political economy as Siéyès' pamphlet: *Qu'est ce que le tiers état?* has for modern politics.

If Proudhon did not conceive the various forms of private property, as, for example, wages, trade, value, price, money, etc., as such, but used these forms of political economy as weapons against political economy, this was quite in accordance with his whole standpoint, as above described and historically justified.

Political economy, which accepts the relationships of private property as human and reasonable relationships, moves in a perpetual contradiction to its fundamental assumption, which is private property, a contradiction analogous to that of theology, which constantly gives a human interpretation to religious ideas, and thereby constantly violates its fundamental assumption, which is the supramundane character of religion. Thus in political economy wages appear at the outset as labour's proportionate share in the product. Wages and the profit of capital exist in the most friendly and apparently human relations, alternately assisting each other. Subsequently it transpired that they stand in the most hostile, in an inverted, relationship towards each other. In the beginning value is apparently determined on rational principles, by the costs of production of an article and by its social utility. Subsequently it transpires that value is a purely accidental determination, which does not need to have any connection at all either with the costs of production or with social utility. The magnitude of wages is in the beginning determined by a free contract between the free worker and the free capitalist. Subsequently it transpires that the worker is compelled to let it be determined, just as the capitalist is compelled to fix it as low as possible. Coercion takes the place of the freedom of the contracting parties. The same observation applies to trade and all the other relations of political economy. Political economists occasionally have an intimation of these contradictions, the development of which forms the principal content of their mutual wrangling. When, however, they become fully aware of them, they proceed to attack private property in one of its partial manifestations, as the falsifier of wages which are rational in themselves, that is, in the ideas they have formed about wages; or of value that is rational in itself, or of commerce that is rational in itself. Thus Adam Smith occasionally attacks the capitalists, Destutt de Tracy attacks the money-changers, Simonde de Sismondi attacks the factory system, Ricardo attacks landed property, and thus almost all political economists attack the non-industrial capitalists who regard property merely as consumable goods.

Sometimes, therefore, the political economists invest economic conditions with a human semblance, that is, when they are attacking a particular abuse, but at other times, which is mostly the case, they interpret these conditions in their strict economic meaning, as distinguished from human conditions. They reel unconsciously in this contradiction.

Now Proudhon has made an end once for all of this unconsciousness. He took seriously the human semblance given to economic conditions and sharply confronted it with their inhuman reality. In all seriousness he accepted the human gloss which the political economists had put upon economic conditions, and sharply compared it with their inhuman reality. He demanded that these conditions should be in reality what they are in fancy. In other words, the ideas which have been formed of them should be abandoned and their veritable inhumanity should be acknowledged. He was therefore consistent in plainly representing private property in its most universal aspect to be the falsifier of economic relationships, and not this or that kind of private property, to a partial degree, as did most of the other political economists. He achieved everything that could be achieved by the criticism of political economy from the standpoint of political economy.

All political economy hitherto has taken as its starting-point the wealth which the movement of private property ostensibly creates for the nations, in order to reach its conclusions in support of private property.

Proudhon starts out from the reverse side, which is sophistically covered up in political economy, that is, from the poverty created by the movement of private property, in order to reach his conclusions, which are unfavourable to private poverty. The first criticism of private property was naturally prompted by the phenomenon which embodies its essence in the most striking and clamorous form, a form which directly violates human feeling—by the phenomenon of poverty.

The critics of Proudhon cannot deny that Proudhon also perceives an inner connection between the facts of poverty and of property, as he proposes to abolish property on account of this connection, in order to abolish poverty. Proudhon has done even more. He has demonstrated in detail how the movement of capital creates poverty. The critics of Proudhon, on the other hand, will not enter into such trivialities. They perceive only that poverty and private property are opposites: which is fairly obvious.

Proletariat and wealth are antitheses. As such they constitute a whole; both are manifestations of the world of private property. The question to be considered is the specific position which both occupy in the antithesis. To describe them as two sides of a whole is not a sufficient explanation. Private property as private property, as wealth, is compelled to preserve its own existence, and along with it that of its antithesis, the proletariat. Private property satisfied in itself is the positive side of the antithesis. The proletariat, on the other hand, is obliged, as proletariat, to abolish itself, and along with it private property, its conditioned antithesis, which makes it the proletariat.

It is a negative side of the antithesis, the internal source of unrest, the disintegrated and disintegrating proletariat.

The possessing class and the proletarian class represent the same human self-estrangement. But the former class feels perfectly satisfied with this self-estrangement, knowing that in this estrangement resides its own power, and possesses therein the semblance of a human existence; the latter class feels itself to be destroyed by the estrangement, perceives therein its impotence and the reality of an inhuman existence.

Within the antithesis, therefore, the owner of private property is the conservative, and the proletarian is the destructive party. From the former proceeds the action of maintaining the antithesis, from the latter the action of destroying it. From the point of view of its national, economic movement, private property is, of course, continually being driven towards its own dissolution, but only by an unconscious development which is independent of it, and which exists against its will, and is limited by the nature of things; only, that is, by creating the proletariat as proletariat, poverty conscious of its own physical and spiritual poverty, and demoralized humanity conscious of its own demoralization and consequently striving against it.

The proletariat fulfils the judgment which private property by the creation of the proletariat suspends over itself, just as it fulfils the judgment which wage-labour suspends over itself in creating alien riches and its own condemnation. If the proletariat triumphs, it does not thereby become the absolute side of society, for it triumphs only by abolishing itself and its opposite. In this way both the proletariat and its conditioned opposite, private property, are done away with.

FRENCH MATERIALISM

The French Enlightenment of the eighteenth century, and especially of French materialism, was not only a struggle against the existing political institutions and against the existing religion and theology, but equally an open and outspoken campaign against all metaphysics, especially that of Descartes, Malebranche, Spinoza, and Leibnitz. Metaphysics was confronted with philosophy, just as Feuerbach, in his first decisive stand against Hegel, opposed sober philosophy to drunken speculation. The metaphysics of the seventeenth century, which was driven from the field by the French Enlightenment, and especially by the French materialism, of the eighteenth century, experienced its victorious and opulent restoration in the German philosophy, and particularly in the speculative German philosophy, of the nineteenth century.

After Hegel had combined it in an ingenious manner with all subsequent metaphysics and with German idealism, and founded a universal realm of metaphysics, the attack on speculative metaphysics and on all metaphysics was once again synonymous, as in the eighteenth century, with an attack on theology. Metaphysics succumbed for good and all to materialism, which itself was now perfected by the work of speculation and coincided with humanism.

French and English socialism and communism represented the materialism which coincided with humanism in the practical sphere, just as Feuerbach represented it in the theoretical sphere.

There are two tendencies of French materialism, one of which derives its origin from Descartes and the other from Locke. The latter is pre-eminently an element in French culture and merges directly into socialism. The former, viz., the mechanical materialism, is absorbed in French natural science. The French materialism which derives directly from Descartes does not concern us particularly, any more than the French school of Newton and French natural science generally.

Only this much need be said. In his physics Descartes invested matter with self-creative power, and he conceived mechanical movement to be its vital act. He separated his physics completely from his metaphysics. Within his physics matter is the only substance, the only basis of being and perceiving.

Mechanical French materialism absorbed the physics of Descartes, while rejecting his metaphysics. His pupils were anti-metaphysicians by profession, that is to say, they were physicians.

This school commences with the doctor Leroy, and reaches its acme with the doctor Cabanis, while the doctor Lamettrie is its centre. Descartes was still living when Leroy transferred to the human soul the Cartesian construction of animals, and explained the soul as a mode of the body and ideas as mechanical movements, similarly to Lamettrie in the eighteenth century. Leroy even believed that Descartes had dissembled his real opinion. Descartes protested. At the end of the eighteenth century Cabanis perfected Cartesian materialism in a work entitled: *Rapport du physic et du moral de l'homme.*

Cartesian materialism exists in France even to this day. It had its great success in mechanical natural science, with which Romanticism will least of all be reproached.

The metaphysics of the seventeenth century, as specially represented for France by Descartes, had materialism for its antagonist from its hour of birth. In person this antagonist confronted

Descartes in the shape of Gassendi, the restorer of Epicurean materialism. French and English materialism always remain in close relationship with Democritus and Epicurus.

Cartesian metaphysics found another antagonist in the English materialist Hobbes. Long after their death, Gassendi and Hobbes triumphed over their opponent at the moment when the former reigned in all the schools of France as the official power.

Voltaire once remarked that the indifference of Frenchmen in the eighteenth century towards Jesuitical and Jansenist quarrels was brought about less by philosophy than by Law's financial speculations. Thus the overthrow of the metaphysics of the seventeenth century can be explained from the materialistic theory of the eighteenth century only in so far as this theoretical movement is itself explicable by the practical shape of the French life of that time. This life was directed to the immediate present, to worldly enjoyment and worldly interests, to the secular world. It was inevitable that anti-theological, anti-metaphysical, materialistic theories should correspond to its anti-theological, anti-metaphysical, its materialistic practice. In practice metaphysics had lost all credit. Here we have only to indicate briefly the course of the theoretical movement.

In the seventeenth century metaphysics had already been provided with a positive, a profane content (*pace* Descartes, Leibnitz etc.). It made discoveries in mathematics, physics, and other definite sciences which appeared to belong to it, but by the beginning of the eighteenth century this semblance had been destroyed. The positive sciences had broken away from it and mapped out their own territory. The whole metaphysical realm consisted in nothing more than creatures of fancy and heavenly things at the precise time when real beings and earthly things were beginning to concentrate all interest upon themselves. Metaphysics had become stale. Helvetius and Condillac were born in the same year that Malebranche and Arnauld, the last great French metaphysicians of the seventeenth century, died.

The man who theoretically destroyed the credit of the meta-physics of the seventeenth century and all metaphysics gener-ally was Pierre Bayle. His weapon was scepticism, forged out of the magic formulas of metaphysics itself. He took Cartesian metaphysics as his immediate starting-point. Just as Feuer-bach in combating speculative theology was driven to combat speculative philosophy, because he perceived in speculation the last support of theology, because he had to force the theo-logians to retreat from fictitious science to crude, repugnant faith, so religious doubt drove Bayle into doubts of the meta-physics which supported this faith. Consequently he subjected metaphysics in its entire historical evolution to criticism. He became its historian in order to write the history of its death. Above all he refuted Spinoza and Leibnitz.

Pierre Bayle not only prepared the way for the acceptance in France of the materialism and philosophy of healthy common science through the sceptical disintegration of metaphysics. He announced the atheistic society which was soon to come into existence, inasmuch as a society of avowed atheists could exist, as an atheist could be an honest man, as man was not degraded by atheism, but by superstition and idolatry.

In the words of a French writer, Pierre Bayle was "the last metaphysician in the sense of the seventeenth and the first philosopher in the sense of the eighteenth century."

In addition to the negative refutation of the theology and meta-physics of the seventeenth century, a positive, anti-metaphysi-cal system was required. A book was wanted which would systematize the practical activities of that time and provide them with a theoretical foundation. Locke's essay on the "Ori-gin of the Human Understanding" came as if summoned from beyond the Channel. It was greeted enthusiastically as an anx-iously awaited guest.

It may be asked: Is Locke perchance a pupil of Spinoza? We would answer. Materialism is the native son of Great Britain. Already her schoolman Duns Scotus asked "whether matter could not think?"

In order to work this miracle, he took refuge in God's omnipotence, that is, he made theology itself preach materialism. Moreover, he was a nominalist. Nominalism is found to be a chief ingredient among English materialists, just as it is the first expression of materialism generally.

The real progenitor of English materialism and of all modern experimental science is Bacon. Natural science was regarded by him as the true science, and physics as the principal part of natural science. Anaxagoras and his homoiomeriæ, Democritus and his atoms, are frequently quoted as his authorities. According to his doctrine, the senses are infallible and the source of all knowledge. All science is based upon experience and consists in subjecting the data furnished by the senses to a rational method of investigation. Induction, analysis, comparison, observation, experiment, are the chief instruments of such a rational method. Among the qualities inherent in matter movement is the first and foremost, not only in the form of mechanical and mathematical movement, but even more as an impulse, a vital spirit, a tension, as a qual (a torture)—to use an expression of Jacob Bohme's—of matter.

In Bacon, as its first creator, materialism still conceals within itself in an ingenuous manner the germs of a many-sided development. On the one hand, the sensuous poetic glamour in which matter is bathed entices the whole personality of man. On the other, the aphoristically formulated doctrine swarms with theological inconsistencies.

In its further development, materialism becomes one-sided. Hobbes is the man who systematizes Baconian materialism. Knowledge based upon the senses loses its poetic bloom, and Becomes the abstract experience of the mathematician. The physical movement is sacrificed to the mechanical or mathematical; geometry is proclaimed as the chief science. Materialism takes to misanthropy. In order to overcome misanthropic, fleshless spiritualism on the latter's own ground, materialism must mortify its own flesh and turn ascetic. It reappears as an intellectual entity, but it also develops all the ruthless consistency of the intellect.

Hobbes, as Bacon's continuator, argues that if the senses furnish men with all knowledge, then concepts and ideas are
nothing but phantoms of the material world more or less di-
vested of their sensual forms. All philosophy can do is to give
these phantoms names. One name may be applied to several
phantoms. There may even be names of names. It would, however, imply a contradiction if, on the one hand, we contended
that all ideas had their origin in the world of senses, and, on
the other hand, that a word was worth more than a word; that
besides the individual beings known to us by our senses, there
existed also beings of a general nature. An immaterial substance is rather the same absurdity as an immaterial body.
Bodies, being, substance are but different terms for the same
reality. One cannot separate thought from matter that thinks.
It is the substratum of all changes. The word infinite is meaningless unless it signifies the capacity of our minds to perform
an endless process of addition. As only material things are
perceptible and knowable, nothing can be known about the
existence of God.

My own existence alone is certain. Every human passion is a
mechanical movement which has a beginning or an end. The
objects of impulse are what are called good. Man is subject to
the same laws of Nature. Power and freedom are identical.

Hobbes had systematized Bacon, without, however, providing
any firmer basis for the latter's fundamental principle, the origin of all knowledge and ideas from the world of the senses.

It was Locke who established the principle of Bacon and
Hobbes in his Essay on the Human Understanding.

Just as Hobbes shattered the theistic prejudices of Baconian
materialism, so Collins, Dodwall, Coward, Hartley, Priestley,
etc. broke down the last theological bars which still obstructed
Locke's sensationalism. At least for materialists, theism became nothing more than a convenient and easy-going way of
getting rid of religion.

We have already noticed at what an opportune time Locke's
work came to the French. Locke had established the philoso-

phy of *bon sens,* of healthy common sense, that is, to express it in a roundabout way, that there are no philosophers other than those of the understanding which is based upon the healthy human senses.

Condillac, who was Locke's immediate pupil and French interpreter, lost no time in turning the Lockeian sensationalism upon the metaphysics of the seventeenth century. He contended that the French had rightly spurned the latter as a clumsy product of the imagination and theological prejudice.

He published a refutation of the systems of Descartes, Spinoza, Leibnitz, and Malebranche. In his work: *L'essai sur l'origine des connaissances humaines,* he developed Locke's ideas and contended that not only the soul, but also the senses, not only the art of fashioning ideas, but also the apparatus of sensual receptivity, are subjects of experience and usage. Consequently, the entire development of man depends upon education and external circumstances. Condillac was only supplanted in the French schools by the eclectic philosophy.

The difference between French and English materialism is the difference between the two nationalities. The French endowed English materialism with wit, with flesh and blood, with eloquence. They invested it with grace and gave it the temperament that was still lacking. They civilized it.

In Helvetius, who likewise took Locke as his starting point, materialism receives its proper French character. He applied it immediately to social life. (Helvetius, *de l'homme.*) Sensual qualities and egoism, enjoyment and enlightened self-interests are the foundations of all morality.

The natural equality of human intelligences, the harmony between the progress of reason and the progress of industry, the natural goodness of mankind, the omnipotence of education are the principal factors in this system.

The writings of Lamettrie exhibit the union of Cartesian and English materialism. Lamettrie utilizes the physics of Descartes down to its utmost detail. His *l'homme machine* is a performance executed on the model of the animal machine of Descartes. In Holbach's *Système de la nature,* the section devoted to physics likewise consists of the synthesis of English and French materialism, just as the section devoted to morals is based essentially on the morality of Helvetius. Robinet *(de la nature),* the French materialist who more than all the others kept in touch with metaphysics, expressly founds himself on Leibnitz.

Of Volney, Dupuis, Diderot, etc., we do not need to speak any more than of the physiocrats, now that we have shown the double derivation of French materialism from the physics of Descartes, Spinoza, Malebranche and Leibnitz. This antagonism could only be realized by Germans after they themselves had come into conflict with speculative metaphysics.

Just as Cartesian materialism branches into natural science, so the other tendency of French materialism merges directly into socialism and communism.

No special acuteness is required to perceive the necessary connection of the original goodness and equally intelligent endowment of men, of the omnipotence of experience, custom and education, the influence of external circumstances on men, the extreme importance of industry, the justification of enjoyment, etc., with communism and socialism.

If man receives all his impressions and forms all his conceptions from the world of sense, and derives his experiences from the world of sense, it follows that the empirical world ought to be so constructed as to offer a wealth of truly human experiences. If enlightened self-interest is the principle of all morality, it follows that the private interests of men ought to coincide with human interests. If man is not free in the materialistic sense, that is to say, is free, not by reason of his negative strength to avoid this and that, but by reason of his positive strength to assert his true individuality, then man must not punish the crimes of individuals, but destroy the anti-social breeding-places of crime, and afford to each person sufficient social scope for the expression of his or her individuality. If man is formed by circumstances, then it is only in society that he develops his real nature, and the strength of his nature must be measured, not with the strength of the isolated individual, but with the strength of society.

These and similar sentences may be found almost word for word in the writings even of the oldest French materialists. This is not the place to criticize them. Significant of the socialist tendency of materialism is Mandeville's (one of the older English pupils of Locke) apology for vice. He shows that vice is indispensable and useful in present-day society. This, however, was no justification for present-day society.

The doctrines of French materialism form the starting-point of Fourier. The followers of Babeuf were crude, uncivilized materialists, but even fully-developed communism derived directly from French materialism.

The latter, in the shape given it by Helvetius, returned to its motherland, to England. On the morality of Helvetius, Bentham founded his system of enlightened self-interest, just as Owen, proceeding from Bentham's system, founded English communism. On being banished to England, the Frenchman Cabet was stimulated by the communistic ideas he found there, and returned to France, to become the most popular, albeit most superficial, representative of communism here.

THE ENGLISH REVOLUTION

Pourquoi la revolution d'Angleterre a-t-elle reussi. Discours sur l'histoire de la revolution d'Angleterre, Paris, 1850.[10]

The object of M. Guizot's pamphlet is to show why Louis Philippe and Guizot's policy ought not to have been overthrown on the 24th February 1848, and how the reprehensible character of the French is to blame for the fact that the July monarchy of 1830 ignominiously collapsed after eighteen years of laborious existence and was not blessed with the security of tenure enjoyed by the English monarchy since 1688.

From this pamphlet it may be seen how even the ablest individuals of the *ancien régime*, how even people who in their own way are not devoid of historical talent have been so completely thrown off their balance by the fatal event of February (1848) as to have lost all historical comprehension, even the comprehension of their former behaviour. Instead of being impelled by the February Revolution to study more closely the wholly different historical conditions, and the wholly different positions occupied respectively by the various classes of society in the French monarchy of 1830 and in the English monarchy of 1688, M. Guizot gets rid of the entire difference between the two situations in a few moral phrases and asserts in conclusion that the policy overthrown on the 24th February "can alone master revolutions, as it can sustain States."

---

10   Why the English Revolution was successful. A lecture on the history of the English Revolution, Paris, 1850.

The question which M. Guizot professes to answer may be precisely formulated as follows: Why has middle-class society developed in England under the form of a constitutional monarchy for a longer period than in France?

The following passage serves to show the nature of M. Guizot's acquaintance with the course of middle-class development in England: "Under the reigns of George I and George II, public opinion veered in another direction; foreign policy ceased to be its chief concern; internal administration, the maintenance of peace, questions of finance, of the colonies, of trade, the development and the struggles of the parliamentary régime, became the dominant preoccupations of the Government and of the public" (p. 168).

M. Guizot discovers only two factors in the reign of William III that are worthy of mention: the maintenance of the equilibrium between Parliament and the Crown, and the maintenance of the European equilibrium by means of the struggle against Louis XIV. Under the Hanoverian dynasty, public opinion suddenly "veered in another direction," nobody knows how and why.

It is obvious that M. Guizot has applied the most banal platitudes of French parliamentary debate to English history, believing he has thereby explained it. Similarly, when he was Minister, M. Guizot imagined he was balancing on his shoulders the pole of equilibrium between Parliament and the Crown, whereas in reality he was only jobbing the whole of the French State and the whole of French society bit by bit to the Jewish financiers of the Paris Bourse.

M. Guizot does not think it worth the trouble to mention that the wars against Louis XIV were purely wars of competition for the destruction of French commerce and of French sea power; that under William III, the rule of the financial middle class received its first sanction through the establishment of the Bank of England, and the introduction of the national debt; that a new upward impetus was given to the manufacturing middle class through the consistent enforcement of the protective fiscal system.

For him only political phrases have importance. He does not even mention that under Queen Anne the ruling parties could only maintain themselves and the constitutional monarchy by forcibly prolonging the life of Parliament to seven years, thus almost entirely destroying popular influence over the government.

Under the Hanoverian dynasty England had already progressed so far as to be able to wage competitive war against France in the modern form. England herself combated France only in America and the East Indies, whilst on the Continent she was content to pay foreign princes like Frederick II to wage war against France. When, therefore, foreign politics assumed another aspect, M. Guizot says: "foreign policy ceased to be a chief concern" and its place was taken by "the maintenance of peace." The extent to which "the development and the struggles of the parliamentary régime became the dominant preoccupation of the Government and of the public" may be inferred from the bribery stories about the Walpole ministry, which at any rate bear a close resemblance to the scandals which came to light under M. Guizot.

Why the English Revolution entered on a more prosperous career than the French Revolution subsequently did is explained by M. Guizot from two causes: first, from the fact that the English Revolution bore a thoroughly religious character, and therefore broke in no way with the traditions of the past, and secondly from the fact that from the outset it did not wear a destructive, but a constructive aspect, Parliament defending the old existing laws against the encroachments of the Crown.

As regards the first point, M. Guizot forgets that the free thought of the French Revolution, which makes him shudder so convulsively, was imported into France from no other country than England. Locke was its father, and in Shaftesbury and Bolingbroke it assumed that lively form which later underwent such a brilliant development in France.

Thus we reach the strange result that the same free thought upon which, according to M. Guizot, the French Revolution came to grief was one of the most essential products of the religious English Revolution.

With respect to the second point, M. Guizot forgets that at the outset the French Revolution was just as conservative as the English, if not more so. Absolutism, especially in the guise which it had latterly assumed in France, was an innovation even there, and against this innovation the parliaments arose and defended the old laws, the *us et coutumes* of the old estates-of-the-realm monarchy. And whereas the first step of the French Revolution was the revival of the Estates General which had been extinct since Henry IV and Louis XIII, the English Revolution has no feature of an equally classical conservative nature to exhibit.

According to M. Guizot, the chief result of the English Revolution was this, that it was made impossible for the king to govern against the will of Parliament and of the House of Commons in Parliament. The entire revolution may be summed up by saying that at the commencement both sides, the Crown and Parliament, overstepped their limits and went too far until under William III they reached the proper equilibrium and neutralized each other. That the subjection of the monarchy was its subjection to the rule of a class M. Guizot deems it superfluous to mention.

Consequently, he does not feel it incumbent on him to ascertain how this class acquired the power necessary to make the Crown its servant. He appears to think that the whole struggle between Charles I and Parliament related to purely political privileges. For what purpose Parliament and the class represented therein needed these privileges we are not told. Neither does M. Guizot refer to the direct interferences of Charles I with free competition, which rendered the commerce and the trade of England increasingly impossible; or the dependence upon Parliament into which Charles fell ever more hopelessly, through his continuous financial distress, the more he tried to defy Parliament. According to M. Guizot, therefore, the whole Revolution is to be explained by the evil intent and religious fanaticism of a few disturbers of the peace who could not content themselves with a moderate freedom. M. Guizot has just as little enlightenment to furnish with regard to the connection of the religious movement with the development of middle-class society. Of course, the Republic was likewise the mere work of a number of ambitious, fanatical, and malevolent spirits. That simultaneously efforts were being made to introduce the Republic in Lisbon, Naples, and Messina, as in England, under the influence of the Dutch example, is a fact which is not mentioned at all.

Although M. Guizot never loses sight of the French Revolution, it does not occur to him that the transition from absolute to constitutional monarchy is everywhere effected only after violent struggles and after passing through the stage of the Republic, and that even then, the old dynasty, being useless, must give way to a usurping collateral branch. Consequently, he has nothing but the most trivial commonplaces to utter respecting the overthrow of the English restored monarchy. He does not even cite the proximate causes: the fears entertained by the great new landowners, who had been created by the Reformation, at the prospect of restoration of Catholicism, when they would have been obliged to surrender all the former Church property which had been stolen, which meant that the ownership of seven-tenths of the entire soil of England would have changed hands; the horror of the trading and industrial middle class at Catholicism, which by no means suited its commerce; the nonchalance with which the Stuarts had sold, for their own advantage and that of the Court nobility, the whole of English industry and commerce, that is, had sold their own country, to the Government of France, which was then maintaining a very dangerous, and in many respects, successful competition with the English.

As M. Guizot everywhere leaves out the most important factors, there is nothing for him to do but to present an extremely inadequate and banal narration of merely political events.

The great riddle for M. Guizot, which he can only solve by pointing to the superior intelligence of the English, the riddle of the conservative character of the English Revolution, is explained by the continuous alliance which united the middle class with the largest section of the great landowners, an alliance that essentially distinguishes the English Revolution from the French Revolution, which destroyed large landed property by parcelling out the soil. This class of large landowners, which had originated under Henry VIII, unlike the French feudal land-ownership in 1789, did not find itself in conflict but rather in complete harmony with the conditions of life of the bourgeoisie. Its land-ownership, in fact, was not feudal, but middle class. On the one hand, it placed at the disposal of the middle class the necessary population to carry on manufactures, and on the other hand, it was able to impart to agriculture a development which corresponded to the state of industry and of commerce. Hence its common interests with the middle class, hence its alliance with the latter.

With the consolidation of the constitutional monarchy in England, English history comes to a full stop, as far as M. Guizot is concerned. All that follows is for him confined to a pleasant sea-saw between Tories and Whigs, and this means the great debate between M. Guizot and M. Thiers.

In reality, however, the colossal development and transformation of commercial society in England began with the consolidation of the English monarchy. Where M. Guizot sees only soft repose and idyllic peace, the most violent conflicts, the most drastic revolutions, were in reality developing. First of all, under the constitutional monarchy manufactures underwent an expansion hitherto undreamed of, in order then to make way for the great industry, the steam-engine, and the gigantic factories. Whole classes of the population disappeared, new classes took their place, with new conditions of life and new needs. A large new middle class emerged; while the old bourgeoisie fought the French Revolution, the new captured the world market. It became so all-powerful that even before the Reform Act placed political power directly in its hands, it had compelled its opponents to legislate almost solely in its interests and according to its needs. It captured direct representation in Parliament and utilized it for the destruction of the last vestiges of real power which remained to landed property.

Lastly, it is at this moment engaged in razing to the ground the splendid structure of the English constitution before which M. Guizot stands in admiration.

And while M. Guizot congratulates the English that among them the noxious growths of French social life, republicanism and socialism, have not undermined the foundation pillars of the unique all-blessing monarchy, the class antagonisms in English society have been developing to a point that is without example in any other country. A middle class without rival in wealth and productive forces confronts a proletariat which is likewise without rival in power and concentration. The tribute which M. Guizot pays to England finally resolves itself into this: that there under the protection of the constitutional monarchy the elements making for social revolution have developed to a far greater extent than in all the other countries of the world put together.

When the threads of English development get entangled in a knot, which he seemingly can no longer cut by more political phrases, M. Guizot takes refuge in religious phrases, in the armed intervention of God. Thus the spirit of God suddenly comes over the Army and prevents Cromwell from proclaiming himself king, etc. M. Guizot saves himself from his conscience through God, and from the profane public through his style.

In fact, it is not merely a case of *les rois s'en vont,* but also of *les capacites de la bourgeoisie s'en vont.*